MODERN TIMES

Modern Ire

E. G. Power

LONGMAN GROUP UK LIMITED,
Longman House, Burnt Mill, Harlow,
Essex CM20 2JE, England
and Associated Companies throughout the world.

Published in the United States of America
by Longman Inc., New York.

First published 1988
Third impression 1993

Set in 11/12 point Baskerville Roman
Printed in Hong Kong
NMW/03

ISBN 0 582 22165 X

British Library Cataloguing in Publication Data
Power, E. G.
    Modern Ireland. — (Modern times).
    1. Ireland — History — 1837–1901
    2. Ireland — History — 20th century
    I. Title   II. Series
    941.508   DA950

    ISBN 0-582-22165-X

Library of Congress Cataloging in Publication Data
Power, E. G.
    Modern Ireland.
    (Modern times)
    Includes index.
    Summary: Traces the history of Ireland from the
1840's to the present day.
    1. Ireland — History — 1837–1901 — Juvenile literature.
2. Ireland — History — 20th century — Juvenile literature.
[1. Ireland — History — 1837–1901   2. Ireland — History —
20th century]   I. Title.   II. Series: Modern times
(Harlow, Essex)
DA951.P68   1988   941.508   87-3521
ISBN 0-582-22165-X

Contents

Prologue

Suppose you went to see Ireland for yourself in the early 1840s. . . .

Since 1800 the journey from London to Dublin had been made easier and more comfortable. A continuous turnpike road (the present A5), engineered by Thomas Telford, stretched from London to Holyhead, crossing the Menai Straits to Anglesey by Telford's suspension bridge, opened in 1826. At the busy port of Holyhead you boarded the paddle-steamer which carried the Royal Mail. This crossed the Irish Sea in about four hours and docked at Kingstown, named in honour of George IV, who visited Ireland in 1821. Close to the harbour, rebuilt in 1836, was the railway station, with a train waiting to take you to Dublin, ten kilometres away. In less than half an hour you were in Westland Row station, and could take a cab to the centre of Dublin.

All these transport improvements had been made because of the Act of Union of 1800, which brought to an end the Irish Parliament in Dublin, and created a new United Kingdom Parliament at West-minster, where 100 MPs for Ireland sat with 558 MPs for England, Wales and Scotland. It was important that Irish MPs should be able to travel quickly between their constituencies and London. A fast postal service was also necessary. Ordinary travellers, like yourself, benefited as well.

1
People and places

Dublin

The main streets of Dublin were busy with all kinds of horse-drawn traffic, and the pavements were crowded with people – street pedlars, tradesmen, country people up for the day, soberly-dressed citizens, ladies and gentlemen of leisure and British Army officers in glittering uniforms. English was the language you heard, and you could easily imagine that you were in London or Edinburgh instead of Ireland.

There were wide streets, fine shops and splendid buildings, such as the Law Courts and the Customs House on the north bank of the River Liffey which flowed through the centre of the city. On the south side of the river you could see the imposing entrance to Trinity College (Dublin University), and across College Green the great pillared front of what had been the Irish Parliament House before the Act of Union. Not very far away stood Dublin Castle, the centre of government, where hundreds of officials and clerks dealt with taxation, trade, justice

Carlisle Bridge, Dublin; drawn about 1820. The building on the right with three figures on top is the old Irish Parliament House

and other matters. At the head of all these was the Under-Secretary. He was responsible, in turn, to the Chief Secretary for Ireland, who was a Minister in Queen Victoria's government.

Dublin Castle also housed the headquarters of the police force, the Irish Constabulary who were stationed in police barracks throughout Ireland. They dealt with ordinary crime but were armed to deal with more serious outbreaks of disorder. Dublin, like other large towns, also had its Army barracks. Regiments recruited and based in Ireland formed an important part of the British Army. On the edge of the city, in Phoenix Park, stood the Viceregal Lodge, the official residence of the Viceroy, the Queen's representative in Ireland.

Dublin had been the capital of Ireland for centuries. In the early 1840s it had a population of about 250,000. As well as being the centre of government it was the main port, with large docks, warehouses and shipyards. There were very few big industries, apart from the Guinness brewery, but many small firms of every trade. Most had between ten and twenty employees – craftsmen, apprentices and unskilled workers. Dublin's beautiful public buildings, the mansions of the gentry and the fine houses of eminent lawyers, doctors and senior Civil Servants contrasted strongly with the overcrowded slums in the older parts of the city.

The countryside

To see the country you could travel by stagecoach or by the 'long cars' of Charles Bianconi. This Italian entrepreneur had started his passenger service in 1815, and by 1842 his open carriages connected 128 towns. The usual fare was about twopence (1p) per mile, much cheaper than on the stagecoaches.

In the north, the midlands, and the south generally, the countryside looked much the same as England in the 1840s, with fenced or hedged fields of grain crops or cattle. Here and there were the country houses where the nobility and gentry who owned the land lived. They were all large houses, three or four storeys high, with blocks of stables and coach-houses. Some were almost like royal palaces. You would see many more two-storey farmhouses, with sheds and outbuildings. These were the homes of tenant farmers – sometimes called 'strong farmers', who had over thirty acres of land which they rented from the landlord. You might pass one of them on the road, in hard-wearing weatherproof clothes with strong leather boots and gaiters, riding or driving a horse and cart.

The commonest houses you would see were the one- or two-roomed thatched cottages of small farmers, or cottiers. People of this class had less than thirty acres of land – only a few fields on which they grew corn or kept cattle, and grew potatoes. They sold the corn or cattle for money to pay their rent to the landlord, and they lived on the potatoes.

There were many even poorer homes, the one-roomed cabins of labourers, who worked for the farmers in exchange for half an acre of land to use as a potato patch. A labourer with a large family might have to rent some con-acre. This was land ready-ploughed for planting potatoes which was let from March until the potato crop was harvested. You could easily recognise the families of the poorer cottiers and labourers by their patched, worn and ragged clothes and bare feet.

You might notice that methods of farming were backward except on the largest farms and on the home farms which the landowners managed themselves. You would see many wooden ploughs instead of the iron ploughs used in England. Farm carts often had heavy solid wheels, and harness might be made of twisted straw rope instead of leather.

Towns

As you travelled you would notice how small the towns were, by English standards. Cork, the largest port on the south coast, had only 80,000 inhabitants, and inland towns were much smaller. Most towns seemed simply to have grown out of the countryside. The approach roads were lined with cabins, the same as those of the farm labourers, and you would notice the smell of wood or peat smoke, just as in the villages. The business life of the towns centred around the weekly markets and the fairs, when cattle, sheep, horses and pigs took over the main streets.

The shops were mostly general stores which sold 'whiskey and porter, potatoes, eggs, salt, calico, linen, black-puddings, buttons, thread and meal'. Industries depended on the produce of the land. There were some woollen mills, leather-tanning works and flour mills. In some towns you would see (and smell) the small breweries and distilleries which processed the farmers' grain into stout and whiskey. You would not see any coal-mines, ironworks or steam-powered textile mills like those in the midlands and north of England. The only exception to this was Belfast.

In Belfast from 1828 onwards mills had been equipped with machines for spinning linen yarn from locally-grown flax. Ten years later the linen industry was thriving. As well as the women and children working in the mills, thousands of men were employed in weaving the cloth in their own homes, in towns and villages near Belfast. In the 1840s a railway, the second to be built in Ireland, ran between Belfast and Lisburn, and Belfast's docks were being extended. Through them linen and farm produce went out and manufactured goods from England and Scotland came in. This growing trade meant profits for businessmen, and more jobs for seamen, dockers and waggoners.

The west

When you reached the western counties bordering the Atlantic coast the scenery was breathtaking. The beauty of the landscape, however,

Curraghs used by Irish fishermen had a light framework covered with tarred canvas

lay in the large areas of mountain and bog, and there was very little fertile land for people to farm. The west had very few strong farmers with large farms. Landlords let out their land by the acre or less, often on the con-acre system, and by growing potatoes people were just able to exist from year to year. In some coastal villages the men went fishing, using the traditional small boats called curraghs. Any family with enough land to keep a cow, or a few pigs and some poultry, was reckoned to be well-off. From these western counties men went every summer to the big farms in the midland and eastern counties, and even to England and Scotland, to earn a few pounds helping with the harvest. This money helped to pay for their con-acre, which their wives and children tended while they were away.

Religion

In the early 1840s, 6.5 million out of Ireland's 8 million people were Roman Catholics. They belonged to a single church, while the 1.5 million Protestants were divided into two main groups. Nearly a million of them were members of the Church of Ireland, which was the twin of the Church of England. Over half a million were Presbyterians, who had connections with the Church of Scotland, a Protestant church organised without bishops and archbishops. There were just 20,000 or so members of other Protestant groups such as Methodists and Quakers.

Catholics, Church of Ireland members and Presbyterians did not each belong to one social class and did not live only in one region of Ireland. Yet you were more likely to find them in some positions and places than in others. A rough and ready guide to what you would most likely find in the 1840s would be like this:

Munster, Leinster and Connacht

Landlords; members of the gentry	Church of Ireland
Men in business and professions; craftsmen in Dublin and larger towns; strong farmers	Church of Ireland or Catholic
Small farmers, cottiers and labourers; shopkeepers and tradesmen	Mostly Catholic

Ulster

Landlords	Church of Ireland
Businessmen; craftsmen; big farmers	Mostly Presbyterian
Small farmers and labourers; manual workers in towns	Catholic, Church of Ireland or Presbyterian

To see how this pattern came about we have to look at earlier history. Ireland had been under the rule of kings of England since 1171. This had begun when Anglo-Norman lords from England had defeated local Gaelic chiefs and set themselves up, with their followers, as rulers of a part of Ireland, mostly in the south and east. These adventurers recognised the kings of England in name but did not feel bound to obey their laws and rules. English kings had direct control only in the larger ports and a stretch of land around Dublin, known as the Pale.

In the sixteenth century the Tudor rulers in England decided to take full control. Any chief or nobleman in Ireland who refused to accept their rule had his lands confiscated and given to a loyal English gentleman. In return the new lord was expected to 'plant' English tenants on at least part of the lands. Henry VIII and Elizabeth I carried through the English reformation which resulted in the establishment of the Church of England. An English law then set up a twin Church of Ireland and the new landlords and their planted tenant farmers and servants automatically became members of this new Protestant Church. By the 1840s their descendants were scattered through the south and east of Ireland with the biggest numbers in Dublin and other large towns.

In the seventeenth century James I began an even more thorough plantation of Ulster. The new lords to whom he gave land there were compelled to bring in tenant farmers. James was king of Scotland as well as England and many of the planted tenants were Scots. They brought with them their Presbyterian religion which was much more bitterly anti-Catholic than the Church of Ireland faith. Because of the thoroughness of the Ulster plantation there were parts of the north-east where Church of Ireland and Presbyterian Church members outnumbered the Catholics.

Religious beliefs were held very strongly by both Protestants and

Catholics in Ireland in the sixteenth and seventeenth centuries. The different clergy looked on each other as rivals or enemies. Young men and women of different religion rarely met socially, and intermarriage was almost unheard-of. By the 1840s active hatred had largely died out, and the descendants of sixteenth- and seventeenth-century Protestant settlers considered themselves as Irish as the Catholics. Catholic and Protestant families of the same social class were generally neighbourly. Even so they were rarely very close friends. Such things as Bible-reading in a devout Protestant household, or the nightly saying of the Rosary by a Catholic family would have been acutely embarrassing to a guest who was not of the same religion.

Language

In the 1840s the majority of people spoke English, but about a quarter of the population still spoke Irish, or Gaelic. Gaelic had once been used all over the country, but as the Gaelic-speaking gentry had been replaced by English landlords it came to be used less and less. It was still widely spoken by illiterate country people in the 1840s, particularly in the west of Ireland, but it was no longer used as a written language. Gaelic manuscripts, histories, legends and poems, dating back to the eighth century, were preserved in museums and libraries, but they interested only a handful of specialists in the history of language.

Even though you were unlikely to hear many people speaking Irish on your travels you could hardly fail to notice the exclusively Irish surnames, such as O'Brien, McCarthy, Murphy and others. There were also typically Irish place names which began with the element Bally- (from the Gaelic, *baile*: town) or Kil- (Gaelic, *cill*: church). These might remind you of the Gaelic origin of most of the people who had settled in Ireland in large numbers in the last two or three centuries before Christ.

2
Politics in the 1840s

Background

Of the many earlier laws which disadvantaged Roman Catholics, two still existed after the Act of Union. First, Catholics in any part of the United Kingdom were not allowed to become MPs, nor judges, nor to hold high rank in the Army, Navy or Civil Service. Second, all occupiers of land had to pay a special kind of tax, called the Tithe, to the Established Church. In Ireland this meant that Catholics had to pay to support the Church of Ireland, and so did Presbyterians.

A Catholic lawyer, Daniel O'Connell, organised a great popular movement to remove the first disability. This was the Catholic Association. In 1829 it achieved success when Parliament passed the Catholic Emancipation Act. This allowed Catholics to become MPs and to occupy the other positions from which they had previously been excluded. O'Connell himself became the first Catholic MP at Westminster and in time others were elected.

In 1838 Parliament met the grievance about tithes by cutting the amount by a quarter. The Tithe Act also stated that the money was to be paid by the landowners instead of the tenant farmers. This reduced friction between the Church of Ireland and Catholic (and Presbyterian) farmers, although they were still contributing money to a Church which was not theirs through the rent paid to the landlord.

In 1840 most Irish MPs belonged to the main United Kingdom political parties at Westminster but O'Connell led a separate group of about twenty-five. They now began to demand that Parliament should repeal the Act of Union and restore a separate Irish Parliament.

The Repeal question

O'Connell's demand was for a completely separate Irish parliament in Dublin, and an Irish government, although Queen Victoria would be acknowledged as Queen of Ireland.

Almost all the MPs who represented British constituencies, regardless of which party they belonged to, were in favour of keeping the Union. Although they knew very little about Ireland they were certain that the Union was the best arrangement, not least because it gave Britain security from foreign attack via Ireland.

British MPs could feel reassured that three-quarters of the MPs for Ireland were also in favour of the Union. These MPs represented the views of Ireland's landlords and wealthy classes, as strict property qualifications still meant that poorer men did not have the vote. The landlords regarded the Union as a protection for their social and economic position, while merchants and rich farmers wanted to keep their trade with Britain. The Irish professional class valued the fact that as citizens of the United Kingdom they could work as doctors, lawyers or Civil Servants anywhere in the British Empire.

The Protestant Churches were agreed on opposition to Repeal. The Church of Ireland expected that it would lose its privileged position if there was an Irish parliament with Catholics having the vote. The Presbyterians would not have objected to the Church of Ireland being weakened but they feared that a Catholic Irish parliament would allow persecution of non-Catholics or even encourage it. Such distrust of Catholics was shown most strongly in Ulster where there was the largest number of Protestants. Every summer traditional parades took place in Belfast, Londonderry and other towns to commemorate the Battle of the Boyne (1690) and other events in the defeat of James II by William III. The Catholic James was king of England for three years until he was driven out by the Protestant William. James hoped to use Ireland as a base to regain the English throne but his armies were defeated there by Ulster Protestants and William's army. William was head of the ruling family of the Netherlands, the House of Orange, and the society which celebrated his victories was called the Orange Order. Its Orangemen members marched every year to show their determination to uphold their religion and their leading position in Ulster.

Since the Act of Union many Protestants in Ulster had lost interest in the Orange Order, because the Union seemed to give them enough of a safeguard. Now they saw the demand for Repeal as a new threat both to their religion and to their trade with Britain. When O'Connell visited Belfast in 1841 the police were unable to guarantee his protection, and one Presbyterian minister summed up the typical Protestant attitude with the words, 'Repeal is but another name for Rebellion'.

O'Connell was admired by the whole Catholic population for his success in winning Catholic Emancipation which earned him the name 'the Liberator'. Outwardly his Repeal Association was as well supported as his Catholic Association had been. Catholics of all classes flocked to vast open-air meetings to hear him speak. Yet many did not feel as strongly about Repeal as they had done about emancipation. Some bishops and priests supported him but others believed that the Union was not in itself harmful to the Catholic Church now that emancipation had been won. Many middle class Catholics and strong

O'Connell (wearing a cloak) addresses a Repeal meeting in September 1843

farmers were doubtful if Repeal would make them any better off. The great mass of small farmers, cottiers and labourers had no vote and no deep interest in politics.

In 1843 the Government banned a huge Repeal meeting due to be held at Clontarf, near Dublin. O'Connell called it off, having always insisted on legal, non-violent action. His supporters had been convinced that mass demonstrations of support for O'Connell would win Repeal, as they had won Catholic emanicipation. Now they were totally disillusioned. Their confidence in O'Connell was gone and they had no confidence in themselves.

Young Ireland

A group of young men in the Repeal Association were critical of O'Connell. Their leader was Thomas Davis, and they were often known as Young Ireland, after the Young Italy movement which at

Davis, Gavan Duffy and Dillon planning The Nation *in Phoenix Park in 1842. The monument in the background of this drawing is to the Duke of Wellington*

that time was fighting for Italian unity and independence. Davis and his friends concentrated on producing a weekly paper, *The Nation*, which they used to gain publicity for their views.

They wanted people to understand why they should support Repeal, instead of simply accepting O'Connell's leadership. They wished to make the people of Ireland see themselves as a distinct nation, with the right, if they chose, not to belong to the United Kingdom. O'Connell was content to reassure Protestants that they had nothing to fear from Repeal but Davis told Protestants that, as Irishmen, they should join in demanding Repeal. Davis himself was an example of a Protestant nationalist. He was descended on his mother's side from seventeenth-century settlers, and his father was an Army officer of Welsh origin. Unlike O'Connell, the Young Irelanders believed that if the United Kingdom parliament refused to repeal the Act of Union, the Irish nation would be justified in using force to win its independence.

Davis called what *The Nation* was doing 'mind-making'. He said that his aim was 'to create a race of men full of a more intensely Irish character'. *The Nation* used heroic incidents from Irish history as the basis for stories, ballads and articles, in an effort to strengthen national identity. O'Connell rejected Gaelic (although he spoke it fluently) while Davis encouraged an interest in the country's ancient language. However, *The Nation* emphasised that everybody should work together for the good of Ireland, no matter when or how their ancestors had come to live there. Davis himself asked, in verse:

'What matter if at different times
Our fathers won the sod?
What matter if at different shrines
We worship the one God?'

The success of *The Nation* was remarkable. One student wrote in to say 'Your articles thrill my heart with fire and fury'. Another reader wrote that *The Nation* made him feel 'as if our dear Ireland was a living thing, whom we must love, honour, and serve'.

To many people, though, the intense patriotism of Davis and his friends seemed too romantic and idealistic. One Young Irelander, James Fintan Lalor, supported the aim of building a united Irish nation, but he also pointed out that in their everyday lives Irish farmers and cottiers thought more about land and rents. No nationalist movement would win lasting support unless it showed practical concern for these issues and backed the desire of peasants to own the land.

All these ideas, which were being argued about in the early 1840s, were hotly debated through the second half of the nineteenth century:

That the people of Ireland formed a distinct nation.
That they should govern themselves through a separate Irish parliament.
That force could be used if necessary to end the Union with Britain.
That Irish farmers should have the right to own the land.

Thomas Davis died at the early age of thirty-one in 1845, and Daniel O'Connell in 1847. By then the question of Repeal and the stirring talk of Young Ireland had taken second place to coping with the major disaster of the late 1840s – the famine.

3

The famine

Reaching the crisis

The population of Ireland almost doubled from about 4.5 million in 1800 to nearly 9 million in 1845. Most of the increase was among the poorest classes, the cottiers and labourers. There was no corresponding development of industry to provide jobs, except in the Belfast area, so most of these extra people needed land to grow their own food. This meant that even small farms were subdivided. In 1845 there were over 300,000 so-called farms of five acres or less. Labourers often had to manage to feed themselves and their families on an acre or even half an acre.

The only way to obtain enough food from such small plots of land was to grow potatoes. In 1845 about 3 million people lived on very little else. Every few years since 1800 there had been local failures of the potato crop, but a well-grown acre of potatoes could feed a family of five for a year. No other crop could do that. In the early 1840s some people could see that the time would come when the increase in population would outstrip the supply of food, even from potatoes.

The famine years 1845–7

In the autumn of 1845 disaster struck, in the form of a new crop disease, called potato blight, for which there was no cure. The disease also affected potatoes in England and Scotland, causing some hardship among the poor. In Ireland almost half the entire crop was lost and the effect was shattering.

The cottiers and labourers were the hardest hit. Their food supply for the next twelve months was halved, and they had no money to buy any other food. The strong farmers were not so seriously affected. Although potatoes were an important part of their diet they did not rely on them. Town workers had to buy more expensive bread or oatmeal instead of potatoes, but those who had regular jobs were

A one-roomed peasant's cabin in Donegal. The large basket is a creel for carrying turf (peat)

generally able to manage. The worst hardship was in the west, where people struggled to survive even in normal times.

In the winter of 1845 and the spring of 1846 conditions were harsh. The Government set up a Relief Commission to distribute £100,000 worth of maize, local committees were formed to provide help, and donations were sent to Ireland from Britain, Canada, India and the United States. By the end of June almost all the maize was used up and people were desperately waiting for the next harvest of potatoes to be ready.

A government official described what he saw happen in County Clare.

'I shall never forget the change in one week in August. On the first occasion, on an official visit of inspection, I had passed over thirty-two miles, thickly studded with potato fields in full bloom. The next time the face of the whole country was changed; the stalk remained bright green but the leaves were all scorched black. It was the work of a night.'

This time, in 1846, almost the whole crop was reduced to rotten pulp, and hundreds of thousands of people faced total starvation. The existing system of poor relief was unable to cope with the sudden increase in the number of paupers. Many flocked to Poor Law workhouses in towns which became hopelessly overcrowded. Overcrowding and malnutrition led to the spread of disease, called 'famine fever'. Whole families, in places whole villages, were wiped out. Local Relief Committees did their best to help, but private charity was not enough.

The Government was reluctant to hand out free food. Ministers believed that whatever was needed to replace the potatoes should be imported and sold in the usual way. They did not realise that in many western districts each family was used to growing its own food and there was no system of transport, food merchants or shops. In any case people had no money to buy food, and no way of earning money. Some were given jobs on special relief works, mostly road-building, but the rate of pay was too low, and the work too hard for people weakened by hunger. A reporter wrote:

> 'Children met you, toiling heavily on stoneheaps, but their burning eyes were senseless and their faces cramped and weasened like stunted old men. Gangs worked, but without a murmur, or a whistle, or a laugh, ghostly, like voiceless shadows.'

At last, in March 1847, the Government decided to start direct feeding of the poor, and set up soup-kitchens. Even then the authorities were determined that only 'deserving' cases should be fed. Anyone who was the tenant of more than a quarter of an acre of land was not allowed free food. As a result, thousands of people gave up their little plots, rather than starve to death. The potato harvest in the autumn of 1847 was good, however, and over the next few years deaths from hunger and disease were reduced.

Effects of the famine

When the census of 1851 was taken, it was found that the population was 6.5 million, almost 2.5 million fewer than before the famine. About 1 million people had died of starvation and disease, and 1.5 million had emigrated to Britain, Canada and the United States.

In the early days of the famine some of the better-off farmers sold their possessions while they still had something to sell, and left. Other people got money to emigrate from relatives already living abroad. One man wrote:

> 'If you don't endeavour to take us out of it, it will be the first news you will hear by some friend, of me and my little family to be lost by hunger, and there are thousands dread they will share the same fate.'

In the latter part of the famine most of those who emigrated were penniless. Their fares were paid by the Poor Law authorities, or by their landlords, and conditions on the emigrant ships were almost unbearable.

A drawing from the Illustrated London News *of May 1851 shows the cramped conditions on an emigrant ship*

Emigration as a way out of poverty became a regular feature of Irish life, continuing long after the famine. Irish families who settled in Britain and America did not lose interest in their homeland. Most of them left relatives behind, sending them money when they could, and keeping in touch by letter. They also read reports of events in Ireland in the newspapers and there was a constant flow of new arrivals to describe current events, first-hand.

Most of the Irish emigrants blamed the British Government for doing too little, too late, to help during the famine. Some of the Young Irelanders even accused the Government of deliberately allowing people to die. The emigrants' own harsh experiences and the opinions of Irish nationalist leaders led many of them to contribute money to anti-British organisations. Some of them were ready also to help personally in schemes to overthrow British rule in Ireland.

PART TWO

4
The land 1850–1900

The pattern of agriculture

Before the famine most agricultural land in Ireland was used to grow grain, mainly for export to Britain, or potatoes for home consumption. By 1850 raising cattle to provide meat and dairy produce for the British market was becoming more important. The prices which farmers got for livestock were good, and remained so generally up to the end of the century, although English dealers began to buy more Danish and New Zealand butter after 1880.

To be profitable a cattle farm requires more land and less labour than an arable farm. The change-over was helped by the dramatic drop in the number of labourers and others because of the famine and emigration. From the 1850s, also, labourers married later in life and had fewer children. Landlords encouraged cattle farming by letting land parcelled out into larger farms.

A typical Irish farmer with a farm of about thirty acres was modestly prosperous in the second half of the nineteenth century. The standard of comfort in his home gradually improved; he could provide his daughter with a dowry, and hope to educate one son, often for the priesthood. One son would remain at home to take over the farm. Other children generally had no choice but to emigrate.

In the west of Ireland conditions did not improve as much after the famine. On some landlords' estates hundreds of cottiers had died or had been evicted and these now became huge cattle farms. These ranches did not employ many people. Elsewhere in the west farms remained too small to support a family, and people relied on money from relatives who had emigrated, or on the earnings of the men who went to England as harvest labourers every summer.

Landlords and tenants

Even before the famine most Irish landlords were not enormously wealthy. The failure of the potato crop meant that many of their tenants could not pay any rent, and landlords also had to bear a large part of the cost of government relief work and feeding schemes. Some landlords themselves bought food to give to the poor, while others provided the passage money for tenants to emigrate. As a result many landlords ran into debt and had to sell their estates. The new owners were generally less considerate to tenants who could not pay their rent, and thousands were evicted. Those landlords who stayed on also evicted many families, for non-payment of rent, and to create larger farms which made more economic sense. Evictions reached a peak of 19,000 in 1850, and then fell to below 2000 by 1855, but remained at below 1000 a year for most years between 1858 and 1878.

These evictions were out of a total of about 600,000 farms. This meant that from 1858 to 1878 only about one in every 600 farmers was evicted each year, and the vast majority of tenants in the second half of the nineteenth century continued in the same farm for several generations. Most farmers, however, did not have a lease of their farms. Instead they were tenants-at-will which meant that they could legally be evicted whenever the landlord chose. This uncertainty of tenure was a major grievance.

Another complaint against landlords was that they spent very little money on improving the farms. Farmhouses, farmyard buildings, land drainage and so on usually had to be provided and maintained at the tenant's expense. This gave rise to a demand for 'tenant right'. Tenant right was often called Ulster Custom, because it was generally accepted by landlords in that province. It was a payment made by the incoming tenant to a farmer who was vacating a farm to compensate him for the money he had spent on improvements. Ulster Custom only worked if the landlord agreed that any new tenant who refused to pay would not be given the farm. A great many landlords outside Ulster put up with this custom, but they did so very unwillingly, which caused ill-feeling between them and their tenants.

Gladstone and the First Land Act

Irish nationalists rebelled against British rule in 1848 and 1867 (see Chapter 8). These rebellions did not have much support from farmers and farm workers, but they had an important effect. In 1869 the Liberal Party came to power in Britain and W. E. Gladstone became Prime Minister. When he took office he announced, 'My mission is to pacify Ireland'. He believed the way to do this was to end grievances over religion and land.

His first step, in 1869, was to disestablish the Church of Ireland, which meant that it was no longer superior to any other churches. No one had to pay tithes any more. This satisfied the complaints of Catholics and Presbyterians about having to support a church to which they did not belong.

Gladstone went on to try to meet the complaints of tenants with his

First Land Act of 1870. This gave farmers security against eviction, except for non-payment of rent. A landlord could still get rid of a tenant simply by increasing the rent so much that he could not pay it. Ulster Custom was also legalised throughout Ireland. The Land Act of 1870 did not make much difference to the majority of farmers, but it showed that Parliament was beginning to try to understand Irish problems, and take action on them.

The Land League

In the late 1870s there were partial failures of the potato crop in the west of Ireland. Bad weather affected the hay and oats, leading to a shortage of food for animals. The hardship was much lighter than during the famine but many of the small farmers could not pay their rents. At the same time there was a slump in the United States economy, and emigrants there were unable to send as much money to their relatives in Ireland. The number of evictions for non-payment of rent increased to over 1000 in 1879, 2000 in 1880, and more than 3000 in 1881. The unexpected hardships and evictions gave rise to the usual forms of peasant retaliation against unpopular landlords – setting fire

A family and their belongings, thrown out of their home, 1888

to hay barns or maiming cattle. In 1879, however, there happened to be a leader who was able to organise more effective action. He was Michael Davitt.

Davitt was the son of a small farmer of County Mayo, who had been evicted in 1852 and went to Lancashire. Michael worked as a child in a cotton mill and lost an arm in an accident. When he grew up he joined the Fenians (see Chapter 8) and spent some time in prison. He was influenced by the writings of the Young Irelanders, and particularly by the idea of Fintan Lalor that nationalism would only succeed if it had the support of Irish farmers. Davitt was back in Mayo in 1879, and set up an organisation of tenant farmers called the Land League. The Land League's slogan was 'The Land for the People', and there were soon branches of the League in other western counties as well as Mayo.

Davitt showed the farmers that if they stood together they could resist eviction. A tenant was to refuse to pay an unreasonably high rent, and if the landlord then evicted him no one else was to take the farm. Then the landlord would get no rent at all. Davitt was greatly helped in organising the Land League by the young nationalist MP Charles Stewart Parnell, and the so-called Land War began.

The Land War was really a test of endurance between the Land League and the landlords who could call on support from the police, the courts and the Army. Against this powerful combination the Land League needed to keep the farmers united. Its most effective weapon was a way of dealing with farmers who took over the land of evicted tenants. The Land League saw to it that they were treated as outcasts. Their neighbours would not speak to them or help their families in any way.

The same method was used against one of the most unpopular men in the west. He was Captain Boycott, the manager of Lord Erne's estates in County Mayo. Local people refused to work for him in Lord Erne's house or on his land. Labourers were brought in from Ulster, protected by hundreds of police and troops, but life became so unbearable for Boycott that he had to leave. From then on the word 'boycott' was used for this sort of action. In this case Lord Erne reduced all rents by a tenth so the boycott was successful.

The Second Land Act and later Acts

When Gladstone became Prime Minister for the second time, in 1880, he decided that something more needed to be done to 'pacify Ireland' and so he persuaded Parliament to pass another Land Act in 1881. Parnell, Davitt and other Land Leaguers were imprisoned for a time (to show that the Government was really still in control) but the power of landlords to decide rents was taken away. The Second Land Act set up a Land Commission to rule on what was a fair rent. Farmers were protected from eviction. If a tenant left a farm willingly he could charge for improvements he had made to it. Another Act, the Arrears

Act, was passed in 1882 to protect tenants who owed rent from previous years.

Tenants all over Ireland made good use of the Land Commission Courts which fixed rents. These Courts were very sympathetic to the farmers and set rents at much lower levels. Many landlords began to find that they could no longer make a satisfactory living and by 1884 over 1000 were ready to sell their land to their tenants. In 1885 the Ashbourne Act created a fund to lend government money to Irish farmers so that they could buy their own farms. Other similar Acts followed, making the terms attractive to both landlords and tenants and by 1917 nearly two-thirds of farmers owned their own land. The people who benefited most from rent reductions and land purchase schemes were the bigger farmers. Small tenants with less land and lower incomes were less able to take advantage of them. Farm labourers did not benefit at all.

Congested districts

Conditions in the west of Ireland did not improve and eventually it was seen that more direct government help was needed. In 1891 a special authority, the Congested Districts Board, was set up. Congested districts were not actually overcrowded, but had a bigger population

Clearing the route for a government-funded railway in County Galway in 1893

than the land could support. Money was spent on building narrow-gauge railways, encouraging cottage industries, and helping inshore fishing, but it made very little real difference.

The early twentieth century

By the early years of the twentieth century the land of Ireland was well on the way to being owned by the farmers themselves, and farming was slowly improving. The Irish Agricultural Organisation Society was helping farmers to set up Co-operative Creameries for better quality butter, to improve livestock and crops and to buy agricultural machinery. However, exports of farm produce went almost entirely to England, where they faced increasing competition from other producers such as Denmark and New Zealand. Most farmers worked their land with family help, so there were few jobs for labourers and there was almost no rural industry. Emigration continued to be the only course open to the children of labourers, and younger sons and daughters of small farmers. Between 1850 and 1900 about three million went to the United States, and thousands more went to Britain or the British Dominions. Many people believed that the Government was not doing enough to develop the use of the land so that young men and women could make a living in Ireland.

5

Towns, trade and industry 1850–1900

Lack of industrial development

The Act of Union of 1800 and an Act of 1824 which abolished customs duties between Britain and Ireland created a free trade area within the whole of the United Kingdom. Goods could pass without restriction in any direction. Money from one area could be freely invested in industry in another. Yet industry did not grow evenly throughout the United Kingdom. It needed places where there were enough people to buy goods, a suitable labour force, and a supply of raw materials.

Ireland had few of these requirements for large-scale industrial development after 1850. The population of 6.5 million in 1851 continued to fall, down to 4.5 million in 1901. Most people were relatively poor, spending most of their incomes on food, little on clothing and almost nothing on household goods or other manufactures. There was little skilled labour. There were no large deposits of coal, iron or other metals. People who did have money to lend preferred to invest it in successful companies in Britain, rather than risk it in new ventures in Ireland. Irish handicraft industries which already existed in 1850 were put out of business by competition from British, factory-made goods. In Ireland, as everywhere in the United Kingdom, cotton goods were bought from Lancashire, woollens from Yorkshire, hardware from the Black Country, pottery from Staffordshire. From 1850 railways and steamships reduced the transport costs of goods mass-produced in distant factories.

Some Irish industries also declined for particular reasons. Tanning and leather production suffered a shortage of raw material as the trade of supplying salt beef for ships changed to that of exporting live cattle. Butter-making and bacon-curing were hit by the growing preference for Danish butter and bacon in England after 1880. Even Irish farmers themselves bought American bacon when it became available in the 1870s, because it was cheaper. Flour-milling was once carried on in small local mills; after 1870 it was done in the ports by big steam mills using cheap American wheat.

Apart from those based in Belfast, the industries which progressed were those which exported a large part of their product. Blarney Woollen Mills, near Cork, was employing 750 workers in the 1890s, and exported most of their output. Whiskey distilleries and breweries also did well, especially the Guinness Brewery in Dublin. A handful of luxury industries continued to thrive, such as Waterford Glass and Belleek China.

Towns and cities

Irish towns were very small by English standards, although they continued to grow in the second half of the nineteenth century. Emigration did not cut their numbers; instead people moved to towns from the countryside hoping for work. Generally they were disappointed because towns such as Cork and Limerick still depended on trade far more than industry. They were ports shipping cattle and dairy produce to England, and importing British clothing, shoes, hardware, furniture, and other commodities. Dublin, the capital city, was unique as the centre of administration for the whole of Ireland, and the port with the shortest sea-route to Britain. It had a population by 1900 of about 300,000. Even then, Dubliners were constantly reminded of the agricultural character of their country by the herds of cattle being driven through the main streets down to the docks.

Belfast was the only city in Ireland that was really an industrial centre, similar to Birmingham or Leeds in England. By 1850 linen manufacture was long-established and was being carried on in steam-powered factories similar to the cotton mills of Lancashire. Most of the

Reeling yarn in Ewart's Mill, Crumlin Road, Belfast

cloth was exported to Britain. In the 1850s the small shipbuilding industry was given a tremendous boost by the establishment of the great shipyard of Harland and Wolff. This was followed in 1879 by the shipyard of Workman, Clark and Co. Almost all the ships were built for British companies, such as the White Star Line.

The big passenger liners of the late nineteenth century required an enormous amount of craft work to fit cabins, lounges, and so on, and wages were lower in Ireland than in English or Scottish shipyards. Hundreds of families from the nearby countryside moved into Belfast for work in the shipyards and in supporting industries such as rope-making. By the beginning of the twentieth century Belfast, with a population of 400,000, had far outgrown Dublin. The coal, iron, and other raw materials for the industries of the Belfast area all had to be imported from Liverpool or Glasgow and the products were sold to Britain. This meant that Belfast businessmen were in contact with England and Scotland more than with towns and cities in Ireland.

Social conditions in Belfast and Dublin

The growth of Belfast into a large industrial city brought with it the usual nineteenth-century drawbacks as well as the benefits. The profits of thriving firms went mostly to the owners, shareholders and senior managers. The ordinary people had jobs, but thousands of workers were sometimes laid off because of a sudden slump in world demand for their products.

The houses where working-class families lived were built in long rows on narrow streets, or cramped together around small unpaved yards. In 1852 only 3000 out of a total of 10,000 houses in Belfast had water laid on, and a satisfactory supply was not provided until the beginning of the twentieth century. The sewerage system was not completed until 1887, and there were still 20,000 houses with no back doors in the 1890s. These conditions led to a great deal of illness. Many men and women who had worked in the linen mills as children suffered from a disease caused by inhaling the flax dust. The unskilled and lowest paid workers suffered most hardship. These generally were the families most recently arrived in Belfast from the rural areas, many of them Catholics.

Conditions for the poor in Dublin were on the whole even worse, and there was much less chance of any sort of regular work. The poor often lived in houses built originally for wealthy people who had since moved to pleasanter homes in the suburbs. In 1900 about 20,000 families lived in single rooms often with no form of heat or water supply. The Public Health Committee discovered one case of 'a room, the four corners of which were let out to tenants, and the landlady lived in the middle'. The death rate in Dublin was about 75 per cent higher than in any other British city. In the early 1900s a labourer's wages in Dublin were about 15 shillings (75p) a week; in Belfast, they were about 20 shillings (£1); in England, about 22 shillings and sixpence (£1 12p).

A street market in the late nineteenth century where the poor of Dublin bought and sold

Trade unions

By the middle of the nineteenth century British skilled workers were
well on the way to obtaining reasonable wages and better working
conditions. The 'new model' trade unions date from 1851, and the
Trades Union Congress, which was able to speak to employers and to
Parliament on behalf of its members, was founded in 1868. British
industry as a whole was expanding and there was often a scarcity of
skilled men. In Ireland on the other hand, even in the Belfast area,
it was only in shipbuilding and engineering that skilled craftsmen were
needed. If they were in a trade union at all, they belonged to branches
of various unions based in England. Irish employers generally disre-
garded their demands and they could easily be sacked and replaced
by unemployed men. In 1894 a separate Irish Trades Congress was
set up, similar to the TUC but representing only 60,000 skilled
workers.

Semi-skilled and unskilled workers in Britain began to build lasting unions after the dockers' and gas-workers' strikes in 1888 and 1889, but those in Ireland remained unorganised. Then, in 1907, the London-based National Union of Dock Labourers sent an agent to Ireland. He was James Larkin and his task was to organise the dockers. He began in Belfast. The employers, not used to meeting organised opposition, were stunned by a series of strikes and granted a small increase in wages. Moving to Dublin in 1908, Larkin organised the dockers, carters and other transport workers there. He led three successful strikes and set up his own Irish Transport and General Workers Union.

About five years earlier, James Connolly had attempted to establish an Irish Socialist party, but had failed and gone to America. He now returned and became an official in the ITGWU. After winning more wage increases, and seeing ITGWU membership grow to 10,000, Larkin challenged William Martin Murphy, a leading Dublin businessman and founder of the Employers' Federation. Workers in Murphy's United Tramways Company were called out on strike at the end of August 1913 and the trial of strength between Larkin's union and the Employers' Federation spread rapidly to other industries and services. By the end of September 25,000 men were either on strike or locked out by their employers. Larkin and Connolly were both arrested, and there was violent fighting between the police and workers. Police brutality led Connolly to protect workers' meetings with a small disciplined force which he named the Irish Citizen Army. With donations from the TUC and other sympathisers in England, the strikers held out until the first months of 1914, when the men were forced by cold, hunger and illness among their families to return to work at their old wages and on condition that they resigned from the ITGWU. Larkin left Ireland later in the year but Connolly remained as the leader of what was left of the Labour movement.

James Connolly by now firmly believed that Ireland would have to be self-governing before there could be a more equal sharing-out of wealth for the working class. Many Irish businessmen also thought that an Irish government would protect their industries from English competition, and help them develop trade links with other countries. But workers and employers in the north-east were not so keen on the idea of an independent Ireland. This was partly because their prosperity was tied to the British economy, but there were other reasons, described in the following chapters.

6

Social and cultural changes 1850–1900

The decline of the Gaelic language

The Gaelic language had already given way to English over most of Ireland when Davis and his friends launched *The Nation* (in English) in 1842, and the famine led to an even faster decline. Many emigrants from the west of Ireland were Gaelic speakers, and anyone who might expect to emigrate had to know English. English was spoken by government officials, by the police, in courts, in business; and it was the language of newspapers, magazines and books. Gaelic was regarded as suitable only for the most backward peasants. Davis remarked that 'the middle classes think it a sign of vulgarity' to speak Gaelic. In 1851 about a quarter of the population of 6.5 million still spoke Gaelic. By 1891 only 680,000 out of 4.7 million used it.

Basic education

When the Government set up the National Board of Education in Ireland in 1831 only two out of every five children were attending a school of any kind. Classes were held in the teacher's house, or in a shed, or in the open in a 'hedge' school. The Board intended to provide 'mixed schools' for children of any religion up to the age of about eleven, but the leaders of the three main Churches objected. Eventually they all came to terms with the Board, which gave money for buildings, teachers and books. Although a child of any religion was allowed to attend any National Primary School, in practice each school was attached to a particular Church, with the local priest, rector, or minister acting as School Manager. At the end of the nineteenth century 65 per cent of pupils under eleven were in schools where all the children and staff were of the same religion.

All the National Schools taught English and used English text-books, and even Gaelic-speaking parents welcomed the chance for their children to learn English. The teaching ignored Irish traditions and culture. Irish history was not taught at all and in geography Ireland was treated simply as the western part of Britain. The 'Class Readers' celebrated British achievements in invention, in civilising the world, and in military and naval success. The National Schools, however, did give children a basic education. In 1851 nearly half the population was illiterate. By 1911 this figure had fallen to one-tenth.

Even if there was not a deliberate plan to destroy Irish culture, as some critics believed, the increase in literacy had a bad effect on Gaelic traditions. It meant that nearly everybody could now read popular English magazines and the latest novels, and these made Irish traditions and ways seem very old-fashioned and dull.

Secondary and university education

Secondary schools in Ireland were also closely connected with one particular Church. Secondary education was reserved for the children of wealthy parents, as fees had to be paid except in the schools run by the Christian Brothers, a Catholic teaching order. After 1879 the Board of Education made grants to secondary schools, and began to award scholarships, so that poor children had a chance, if they were very clever, to be educated beyond the primary stage.

University education was almost non-existent in 1850, except for wealthy Protestants who could attend Dublin University (Trinity College) which dated from the reign of Elizabeth I. Three new university colleges, called Queen's Colleges, had been set up by the Government in 1848. They accepted students of any religion, but provided no courses in religious studies. They were branded as 'Godless Colleges' by the Catholic Archbishop, John McHale, and Catholic students were strongly advised not to attend them. The only one which was reasonably well-attended was Queen's College, Belfast, with mainly Church of Ireland and Presbyterian students.

In 1879 a new plan created the Royal University. This merely conducted degree examinations which could be taken by any candidates whether they had attended one of the existing colleges or had studied privately. This gave way in 1908 to the National University of Ireland, with colleges in Dublin, Cork and Galway. Queen's College, Belfast, was given separate status as Queen's University. Trinity College, Dublin, continued its aloof existence as the University of the one-time ruling class.

Religious change

There was little change in the proportions of people of different religions in Ireland between 1850 and the end of the century. Catholics made up about three-quarters of the population. Church of Ireland Protestants made up about half of the remaining quarter, or about 12½ per cent. Nearly two-thirds of these lived in Ulster. Presbyterians, almost all in the north-east, amounted to about 10 per cent. The remaining $2\frac{1}{2}$ per cent consisted of other non-Catholic groups: Methodists, Baptists, etc., and Jews.

There was almost no intermarriage between religions, or conversions, although there was little active hostility between ordinary people over religion, except in Ulster at times. The non-Catholic groups tended to co-operate with each other rather more and to be more regular in church-going and other religious observances than in England. They felt it right to show Catholic neighbours that Protestants were also devout Christians.

The Catholic Church in Ireland became stronger as the Protestant Church of Ireland became weaker. The single most important change came with Gladstone's Disestablishment Act in 1869, by which the Church of Ireland lost its status and a good deal of its income. It was now merely one among several religions and only a poor second to the Catholic Church in numbers. The Land Acts reduced the importance of the Church of Ireland's leading members, the landlords. The spread of democracy through various nineteenth-century Parliamentary Reform Acts increased the number of Catholic voters. The establishment of popularly elected County Councils and District Councils in 1898 meant that these became mainly Catholic authorities who took over the management of local affairs, previously in the hands of the Protestant gentry.

The Catholic Church also became stronger through becoming better organised. This was mainly through the work of Paul Cullen, Archbishop of Dublin from 1852 to 1878. He became Ireland's first Cardinal in 1866, a sign that the Papacy recognised the importance of the Roman Catholic Church in Ireland. The clergy were encouraged to be more active, and their numbers increased from 5000 priests, monks and nuns in 1850 to 14,000 in 1900. Many large new churches were built, the Christian Brothers and other teaching and charitable orders were supported, and the Temperance Movement (restricting alcoholic drinks) was encouraged. As Cardinal Cullen's work was continued after his death, the Catholic population became more proudly Catholic than ever before. Bishops and priests increasingly warned their people about the dangers of atheistic, irreligious and immoral ideas being spread by newspapers, magazines and books from England. They were therefore very willing to support any movement against English, modern ways and attitudes.

The Presbyterian Church also became stronger during the second half of the nineteenth century. The Presbyterians in the north-east, like the Catholics in the rest of Ireland, benefited from the wider right to vote in parliamentary and local government elections. The Land Acts reduced the control of Church of Ireland landlords over Presbyterian tenant farmers in Ulster. The Presbyterian religion, which had been made up of a number of different groups, was unified from 1840 onwards, under the General Assembly of the Presbyterian Church. There followed in 1859 a great Revivalist movement which set out to strengthen the spiritual and moral lives of individuals but tended also to increase mockery and hatred of Roman Catholic beliefs and religious practices.

The Gaelic Revival

In the 1840s Thomas Davis had hoped to counteract English influence by developing a common Irish culture which would combine the Gaelic heritage with elements of later Danish, Norman, English and Scottish tradition. Forty years later there was an attempt to revive an exclusively Gaelic culture.

The first sign of this Gaelic Revival was the founding of the Gaelic Athletic Association in 1884 by Michael Cusack. The GAA took two traditional Irish games, football and hurling, which were still being played between village teams, without generally recognised rules or marked-out pitches. Rules were drawn up, and proper clubs formed. Matches were held at parish and county level, and within three years the first All-Ireland Final was played. Support for the GAA came from Archbishop T. W. Croke, who wrote to Cusack

> 'We are daily importing from England, not only her manufactured goods . . . but, together with her fashions, her accents, her vicious literature, her music, her dances and her manifold mannerisms, her games also and her pastimes, to the utter discredit of our own grand national sports.'

The GAA believed in keeping Gaelic culture pure. Right from the start its rules laid down that anyone who played cricket, rugby or other 'foreign' games would not be allowed to take part in Gaelic football or hurling.

Another aspect of the Gaelic Revival was an effort to revive the language. For many years a few university linguists had been studying Gaelic literature – poetry written as long ago as the eighth century and even earlier stories and legends. In 1878 Standish O'Grady translated the earliest legends and published them as *The History of Ireland: the Heroic Period*. This showed people in Ireland for the first time that there were Gaelic tales comparable to the legends of ancient Greece or the British stories of King Arthur. Soon many popular versions of the legends were being published. There was also a revival of interest in the folklore and music of the few Gaelic-speaking areas left in the west of Ireland. A group of poets, novelists and playwrights, including W. B. Yeats and J. M. Synge, began to produce work written in English, but with the turns of phrase and Irish dialect words used by the peasants.

In 1893 Douglas Hyde and Eoin MacNeill founded the Gaelic League, to restore the Gaelic language as the everyday speech of the people. The League arranged classes and published textbooks. Pressure from the League made the Board of Education allow Gaelic to be taught in schools, and in 1909 Gaelic was made compulsory for

Faughs (Dublin) hurling team, 1900–1904

entrants to the National University. In spite of this, very few people began to use Gaelic as their everyday language, although there was great interest in Irish literature and early Irish history, particularly among young Catholics, who also showed most enthusiasm for the national games, songs, and dances.

Although many of the Gaelic writers were Protestants, the landlord class as a whole took no interest in the attempt to revive Gaelic culture. The Protestants of Ulster showed more concern, but wanted to oppose, not support it. Many of the stories of ancient Gaelic kings and warriors were set in Ulster, but this only underlined the point that the Protestants living there were a different people. Some Presbyterians even rejected the term 'Irish' and began to speak of themselves as 'Ulster Scots', to emphasise the distinction between themselves and the 'native' Irish. This gave an added boost to the Orange Order (see page 8) which continued to gain members, including many from the upper and middle classes who had previously not been much involved in its activities.

As the Catholic Church became more powerful, and some Catholics seemed set on reviving Gaelic culture and language, Protestants, especially in Ulster, became more anxious about their future. Their worries were not lessened by the way political affairs were going in the United Kingdom.

This Unionist postcard emphasised the separate origins of Ulster Protestants

7
Parliamentary Nationalism

The demand for Home Rule

After O'Connell's death in 1847 and the collapse of the Repeal movement, the Irish MPs at Westminster remained divided between Whigs and Tories, although there was a small separate Tenant League group for a while during the 1850s.

A new attempt to organise Irish Nationalist MPs into a separate party came in 1870, when Isaac Butt founded the Home Government Association, soon to become the Home Rule League. Home Rule meant much less than Repeal. There would be a separate Irish parliament in Dublin, but it would have power only to deal with internal affairs. Foreign affairs, security and overseas trade would still be controlled by the United Kingdom Parliament. The idea of Home Rule caught on amongst voters in Ireland, and in the 1874 election fifty-nine Home Rule MPs were elected, the other Irish MPs being Tories or Liberals.

The Home Rulers could have formed a strong bloc, but Isaac Butt was uncertain of how to go about getting Home Rule. He was too gentlemanly to make a nuisance of himself. Charles Stewart Parnell, a Protestant landowner elected as MP in 1875, had no such qualms.

Parnell and a small group of Home Rulers decided that, if the House of Commons refused to discuss Irish problems, they would see to it that nothing else was discussed sensibly. Their plan, called Obstructionism, was to make long speeches one after another, keeping debates going day and night. This made nonsense of the Government's timetable of subjects to be debated and infuriated other MPs, but it delighted the supporters of Home Rule in Ireland.

In 1880 the Irish Home Rule Party had sixty-one MPs and Parnell was elected leader, after the death of Isaac Butt. It was now a well-organised party, able to do more than simply disrupt the work of the House of Commons, and it went on growing more powerful under Parnell's dynamic leadership. In Ireland its members worked hand-in-glove with the Land League (see page 19). Parnell also had the approval of the extremist Fenian Brotherhood (see Chapter 8), massive donations from Irish organisations in the United States, and increasing support from the Catholic bishops and clergy. No wonder he came to be called the 'Uncrowned King of Ireland', as hopes rose that Home Rule was becoming inevitable.

The 1885 election

The general election of 1885 saw eighty-five Home Rule candidates elected in Ireland (and one Home Rule MP in Liverpool). In this election there were three main parties in Ireland; Home Rule, Conservative, and Liberal. Both the Conservatives and the Liberals were against Home Rule. Voters who were in favour of Home Rule all voted for Home Rule candidates; but those who were against Home Rule split votes between Conservatives and Liberals. In some places this let in the Home Rule candidate, even though more voters were against Home Rule than for it.

The effect was most noticeable in Ulster. There, Home Rulers won seventeen seats out of a total of thirty-three; previously they had only three seats. Protestants in Ulster were very alarmed at this, and the Orange Order gained many new members from among landowners and businessmen. These quickly took steps to make sure that the votes against Home Rule would not be split again.

The first Home Rule Bill 1886

The result of the 1885 election impressed the Liberal Prime Minister, W. E. Gladstone. In 1886 he announced that he would introduce a Bill to give Home Rule to Ireland. This would have been passed by the Commons if the Liberal Party had remained united behind Gladstone, but ninety-three Liberal MPs broke away to form a separate Liberal Unionist Party led by Joseph Chamberlain. They were enough, voting with the Conservatives, to defeat the Home Rule Bill.

In Ulster the Liberal Unionists, urged on by the Orange Order, began to co-operate with the Conservatives. They agreed not to oppose each other in future parliamentary elections. This meant that there was now a single Unionist Party in Ireland, with the main aim of opposing Home Rule.

The British Conservatives now took a much stronger line against Home Rule, influenced by one of their younger leaders, Lord Randolph Churchill. He thought that if he played on Ulster Protestants' fears his party would win more votes in Britain. 'I decided' he wrote, 'the Orange card would be the one to play.' He visited Ulster to reassure Unionists that they would get firm support in Britain, and he encouraged resistance with the slogan 'Ulster will fight and Ulster will be right'.

Gladstone held another general election in 1886, after the defeat of

A picture from the Illustrated London News *of Gladstone introducing the first Home Rule Bill to the House of Commons, 8 April 1886*

his Home Rule Bill. This time there was a straight fight in Ulster between Home Rule and Unionist candidates. The Unionists won seventeen seats. In the United Kingdom as a whole there was a large majority of Conservative and Liberal Unionist MPs, and Gladstone therefore resigned.

The fall of Parnell and the Second Home Rule Bill 1892

It was clear that the Home Rule Party had as much support as it could ever hope for in Ireland. Home Rule would depend on how well the Liberal Party could do against the Conservatives and Liberal Unionists in elections in British constituencies. Some Irish nationalists were resentful that Ireland's future seemed to depend on the outcome of voting in Britain, but most people were prepared to wait until there was a majority in favour of Home Rule.

In 1892 the leadership of Parnell was badly damaged because of events in his private life. He was living with Mrs Kitty O'Shea, the wife of a former Home Rule MP. O'Shea and his wife had in fact been leading separate lives for some years, but it was only in 1890 that he sued for divorce. Parnell was named as co-respondent, and the evidence in the trial was reported at length in the press in Britain and Ireland.

Nonconformists in Britain, regarded as the main strength of the Liberal Party, were outraged, and Gladstone warned the Home Rule Party that Parnell would have to give up the leadership, or lose Liberal support. Catholic opinion in Ireland was also shocked, and condemned Parnell, and the Home Rule Party split. Even after Parnell's death in 1891 the split continued until 1900, causing a great deal of bitterness within the Home Rule movement.

In spite of all this, the Liberals won the 1892 election, and Gladstone introduced his Second Home Rule Bill, again raising fears in Ulster and hopes in the rest of Ireland. This time the Bill was passed by the House of Commons, but was heavily defeated in the House of Lords, which was mainly composed of Conservative peers.

The Third Home Rule Bill 1912

After the general election of 1910 the Liberal Government needed support from the Irish Home Rule MPs. In return for this, their leader, John Redmond, asked that the Liberal Party should bring in another Home Rule Bill. Success seemed more likely when the power of the House of Lords to prevent a bill from becoming law was ended in 1911. In future the Lords could only delay a bill for two years. In 1912 the Liberal Prime Minister, H. H. Asquith, introduced the Third Home Rule Bill. Even if the House of Lords rejected it, it was certain to become law in 1914. There was no way in which the Conservatives and Unionists could prevent it; at least no parliamentary way.

The Conservative Party leader, Bonar Law, hinted though at other ways of resistance when he said 'there are stronger influences than parliamentary majorities'. In another speech he declared 'I can imagine no length of resistance to which Ulster can go in which I should not be prepared to support them'. Events in Ulster showed that these were not empty words.

Resistance in Ulster

The leaders of the Ulster Unionists were James Craig, an Ulster businessman who had served in the British Army during the Boer War, and Sir Edward Carson, a well-known Dublin lawyer. They drew up a declaration called the Ulster Covenant. Those who signed it (some in their own blood) pledged to defend 'our cherished position of equal citizenship in the United Kingdom; to defeat the present conspiracy to set up a home rule parliament in Ireland', and, if one were to be set up, 'to refuse to recognise its authority'.

On 28 September 1912 there was an impressive mass demonstration

A motor cycle section of Ulster Volunteers. Not all Volunteers were so well equipped

of support. After religious services, thousands of men signed the Covenant in Belfast City Hall, and similar ceremonies were held all over Ulster. Carson and Craig raised a private army, the Ulster Volunteer Force, to resist any use of force by the Government. They set up an organisation by which the Unionists could rule Ulster themselves, rather than submit to a Home Rule parliament in Dublin. They hoped that these steps would make Asquith withdraw the Home Rule Bill.

Growing tension

In Dublin John Redmond was certain that Asquith could not back down, but others were not so sure. Professor Eoin MacNeill, one of the founders of the Gaelic League, spoke out for a nationalist force to counterbalance the Ulster Volunteers, and this led to the formation of the Irish Volunteers in November 1913. John Redmond at first remained aloof, but as popular support for the Irish Volunteers increased, he took a share in their organisation. This led to a further wave of recruitment. By 1914 the Irish Volunteers had 180,000 men, about twice the number of the Ulster Volunteers.

In 1914 the threat of civil war loomed over the United Kingdom. There was bitter division between Conservatives, who saw Home Rule as an attack on the British constitution and the first step in the collapse of the British Empire, and Liberals who condemned Conservative support for the rebellious Ulster Unionists as a denial of the authority of parliament.

In Ireland, Unionists saw their deep-rooted fears about to become reality. They faced domination by people they had been brought up to look on as inferior with an unacceptable religion and a backward economy. There was no need to highlight the arguments against Home Rule; the most widely-used slogan simply stated 'We will not have Home Rule'. To the majority of Irish Catholics, and indeed some Protestants, the promise of freedom and justice for Ireland through Home Rule now looked as if it might be snatched away at the last moment.

The search for a solution

As Prime Minister, Asquith had three courses open to him. He could give in to Unionist pressure and withdraw the Bill. This would be political suicide for himself and the Liberal Party. Secondly he could try to force Home Rule on Ulster. In March 1914 the War Office planned to move troops from the Army base at the Curragh Camp in Kildare to Ulster. Sixty cavalry officers, some of them Ulstermen, said that they would resign if ordered to take action against the Ulster Unionists. This so-called 'Curragh Mutiny' showed Asquith that he could not fully count on the loyalty of the Army in dealing with opposition in Ulster.

A third possibility was to find some kind of compromise which would partly satisfy both Unionists and Nationalists. In 1912 a Liberal MP, Thomas Agar-Robartes, had put forward the idea of Partition – dividing Ireland in two. Ulster or some part of it would remain under direct rule from Westminster, and the rest of Ireland would be ruled by a Home Rule parliament. The Unionists reluctantly came to accept this, but Redmond insisted that Ireland should not be divided. During 1914 Asquith put various proposals for Partition to Carson and Redmond, but none was acceptable to both leaders. In July 1914 King George V called a conference of British and Irish politicians at Buckingham Palace, but still no compromise was reached and the conference broke up on 24 July.

Two days later the Irish Volunteers landed a shipment of arms from Germany at Howth, just outside Dublin. This matched a cargo of weapons, also from Germany, which the Ulster Volunteers had landed at Larne in April. After failing to prevent the landing of the guns at Howth, British troops fired on a jeering crowd in Dublin, killing three people and wounding thirty-two.

This critical situation was suddenly transformed two days later by the assassination of the Archduke of Austria at Sarajevo, followed by the outbreak of the First World War. The war in Europe ended the danger of civil war in the United Kingdom. The Liberals and Conservatives made a political truce. Redmond and Carson agreed to stop arguing and to help the British war effort. The Third Home Rule Bill was actually signed by George V, but it was agreed that it should not be put into effect until the fighting was over.

8

Armed rebellion

The warlike tradition and the Young Ireland rebellion

There was a long history of armed resistance to the rule of English kings in Ireland. From the reign of Elizabeth I to the end of the seventeenth century this was led by the Irish nobles and gentry, often with Spanish or French help. By about 1700 most of the aristocratic leaders had been crushed and a century of repression followed. Then came the rebellion of 1798, partly inspired by the ideals of the French Revolution, and partly a Catholic peasants' revolt. This uprising led the British Government to suggest the Union which was accepted by the Protestant landlords.

In *The Nation* Thomas Davis encouraged new pride in the gallantry of those who had fought against England, calling them heroes, not rebels to be ashamed of. One of the most popular ballads published in *The Nation* began:

> 'Who fears to speak of Ninety-eight?
> Who blushes at the name?'

Davis and the Young Irelanders believed that, like any other nation, the Irish had the right to use armed force to achieve independence. It was on this principle that they broke away from O'Connell and his Repeal Association.

In 1848, three years after Davis had died, some of the Young Irelanders made a pathetic attempt at rebellion. They had almost no organisation, guns or equipment. People were only just beginning to recover from the effects of the famine, and government agents kept the authorities informed of the plans. *The Nation* was banned. The only military action was a minor skirmish with the police at Ballingarry, in County Tipperary. Some of the leaders were captured and transported for life. A few escaped to France or America. One of these was James Stephens.

The origins of the IRB

James Stephens returned to Ireland in 1856 and went on a 5000-kilometre walking tour of southern and western districts, assessing the attitude of the people. He found that most people accepted the Union, and were interested only in rents, lack of employment and social reforms. He estimated that if a rebellion were not attempted within ten years it would be too late to achieve anything.

Stephens and his supporters therefore began to plan a rebellion to establish a separate Irish Republic. Because of the famine there were hundreds of thousands of Irish emigrants in the United States. These could contribute money to buy the arms and equipment necessary for a successful rebellion, and the United States was a neutral country where organisers could meet without fear of arrest.

In 1858 Stephens founded the Irish Republican Brotherhood in Dublin, while his friend, John O'Mahony, set up a parallel society in the United States which he called the Fenian Brotherhood. He coined the name Fenian from the Fianna, a legendary group of Gaelic warriors.

In Ireland those who joined the IRB were organised in separate 'circles' and only the head of each circle was to know the identity of the leaders. This was to prevent government spies from uncovering the organisation, although it became impossible to preserve secrecy as the date set for the rebellion, 1865, drew near. In addition, there were government agents among the leaders in Ireland and in the United States.

The Catholic bishops and clergy were very much against secret oath-bound societies and denounced Fenianism as sinful, but most members drew a clear line between the need to obey the Church in religious and moral matters and the need to stand by their brothers in the Republican Brotherhood.

Irish MPs also spoke out against the Fenians because they ridiculed the hope of ever gaining Irish freedom through parliamentary activity. As the majority of rank-and-file Fenians were labourers, peasants, and unskilled workmen, most middle class people feared that they were out-and-out revolutionaries who would attack property and religion and begin a reign of terror, as in the French Revolution.

The Fenian Rising 1867

The years 1865 and 1866 passed, but disagreements and lack of weapons prevented any general uprising. The British authorities kept up a constant pressure, closing down the Fenian paper, the *Irish People*, arresting leaders, and scattering small groups found drilling and marching.

Late in 1866 Stephens was replaced as leader of the IRB by Colonel T. J. Kelly, who had fought in the Federal Army during the American Civil War. Kelly planned the rising for February 1867. First the

Irish police hunting Fenians in March 1867. Their work was made easier by an unusually late snowfall

Fenians were to capture the arms depot at Chester Castle, but this attempt failed and the rebellion was put off until the night of 5–6 March.

As usual, the authorities were informed by their agents, and many key men in the Fenian organisation were arrested just before the set date. Thousands of men turned out under their local leaders, but in most places the armed police were able to disperse or capture them without much bloodshed. In all, only about a dozen people were killed. The Irish Constabulary were awarded the prefix 'Royal' for their work in suppressing the rebellion.

The authorities treated those who were captured leniently. There were no executions and few very long prison sentences. In September Colonel Kelly was arrested in Manchester and about thirty local Fenians attacked a prison van trying to rescue him. They succeeded,

Fenians attempt to rescue Kelly from the prison van in Manchester, September 1867

but only by shooting dead the police sergeant guarding the van. Later, three men, Allen, Larkin and O'Brien, were tried and hanged for his murder. They became known as the Manchester Martyrs.

The effects of the rebellion

The execution of the Manchester Martyrs brought to life the small ember of national feeling among Irish people accustomed to thinking merely in terms of land reforms, social improvement and religious equality. The Fenians were prepared to die for Ireland. The Irish Parliamentary Party's paper printed the song which echoed the words of the Manchester Martyrs when sentence was passed on them,

> "God Save Ireland', said the heroes
> God Save Ireland say we all.'

Isaac Butt (later the founder of Home Rule) devoted himself to securing the release of imprisoned Fenians. Charles Stewart Parnell shocked the House of Commons by defending the Manchester Martyrs in a sharp exchange of words with the Home Secretary.

The Fenian movement also began to bring home to English people that their lives could be affected by the Union. Up to 1867, violent opposition to the Union had taken place only in Ireland. In 1867 it was realised that there were Fenians among the Irish who had settled in England and Scotland. They had attempted the capture of Chester Castle, and had carried out the rescue of Colonel Kelly in Manchester. Later in 1867 an explosion during an attempt to free a Fenian prisoner from Clerkenwell gaol in London resulted in twelve civilian deaths and many injuries. When Gladstone began his work 'to pacify Ireland' in 1868, he said that it was the Fenians' deeds which had convinced him that something should be done to satisfy Irish grievances.

The secret work of the IRB

Gladstone's moves over religion, land, and Home Rule created the prospect of eventual self-government for Ireland by peaceful means, but the IRB and its extreme methods continued to exist. After the many betrayals by informers in the 1860s it became a much more select and secret organisation, making no public statements and attempting no mass recruitment. This great secrecy was so effective that, by the end of the nineteenth century, the British authorities believed that the IRB was dead.

In fact, it was very much alive. Its few members were dedicated to complete independence, not Home Rule, and believed that armed rebellion was the only way in which it could be achieved. More important, these members were often key men in other organisations such as the Gaelic Athletic Association and the Gaelic League.

The formation of the Irish Volunteers in 1913 provided the IRB with a unique opportunity. Members of the IRB were quick to join and get themselves promoted to high rank. Thousands of men were trained and armed openly, with the approval of recognised political leaders. The problem which the Fenians had in the 1860s of creating a large, disciplined force in total secrecy no longer existed.

The war, declared in 1914, was also welcomed by the IRB. It was an old saying that 'England's difficulty is Ireland's opportunity', and soon after the outbreak of the war the Military Council of the IRB took the decision to start a rebellion while the Government's attention was focused on Europe.

9

The Easter Rising

Plans for rebellion

When Britain declared war on Germany in 1914, thousands of Ulster Volunteers and Irish Volunteers responded to the call of Carson and Redmond to serve their King and Country. The Catholics who joined the British Army saw no contradiction in serving the King and still wanting Home Rule when the war ended. About 12,000 Irish Volunteers, however, followed their founder, MacNeill, who believed that they should remain in Ireland to guarantee Home Rule.

These men saw the war as a quarrel between Britain and Germany which had nothing to do with Ireland. James Connolly and his Citizen Army (see page 26) took the same neutral attitude, and a large banner was displayed on Liberty Hall, the trade union headquarters in Dublin, which read: 'We serve neither King nor Kaiser, but Ireland'. Another group which took a neutral stand was a small political party called Sinn Fein ('We ourselves') which had been founded by a Dublin journalist, Arthur Griffith, in 1905.

The Government disliked these groups and the parades held by the Irish Volunteers and the Citizen Army, but they thought it better to ignore them while the vast majority of Irish people seemed to support the war effort and recruiting for the British Army was going well.

The Government's disregard of opposition exactly suited the Military Council of the IRB. This included Tom Clarke, an old Fenian released from jail in 1898, and Patrick Pearse, a young teacher and writer, who was on the staff of MacNeill's Volunteers. The IRB leaders told Connolly of their plans in January 1916 and they fixed on Easter Day, 23 April, as the date for rebellion. They sent agents to America to raise money in order to buy guns and ammunition from Germany. Roger Casement went to Germany to arrange for the shipment of the arms. He also tried to persuade prisoners-of-war from Irish Regiments to agree to be shipped to Ireland to take part in the rebellion, but without success.

Up to 21 April no one, except Connolly and the IRB leaders themselves, knew of the plans. Only then did Pearse inform MacNeill that 20,000 rifles and ammunition were due to arrive at Tralee, in the south-west, and that a rebellion had been planned. MacNeill knew that the arms could not be landed in complete secrecy. As soon as the authorities found out he would be arrested and the Volunteer organisation crushed. To prevent the collapse of the Volunteers, MacNeill therefore agreed to give orders for the Volunteers to mobilise on Easter Day and accepted that the Rising should go ahead under Pearse's command.

Alarming news soon reached Dublin. The German ship, *Aud*, flying the Norwegian flag, had been intercepted by a British patrol boat and the arms cargo had gone to the bottom of the sea when the captain scuttled his ship. At the same time, Roger Casement, landing from a German U-Boat, had been arrested by the local RIC.

The authorities in Dublin Castle believed that these two events must mean the collapse of a planned rebellion. This view was confirmed when MacNeill issued a notice on Easter Sunday, 23 April, cancelling all Volunteer parades for that day. MacNeill did so because he considered that it would be madness to rebel without the necessary arms; but Pearse and his comrades met on Easter Sunday and decided that the Rising must go ahead. Pearse sent messages all over Ireland cancelling MacNeill's cancellation notice and ordering all Volunteers to parade fully equipped on Monday 24 April. In some places local Volunteer commanders decided to wait until they received further instructions, and many of those who accepted Pearse's order were unable to assemble all their men. Only in Dublin itself was there a full turn-out on Easter Monday morning. The loss of the arms and ammunition on the *Aud*, and the last-minute changes in orders, reduced the chance of a successful rebellion to nothing. Pearse and the others now only wanted to set a mark for a later generation to aim at. They knew the rising could not succeed. Connolly remarked as they set off from Liberty Hall, 'We are going out to be slaughtered'.

Easter week 1916

Citizens and police in Dublin, used to parades and marches by the Volunteers and Citizen Army, assumed that the men marching off from Liberty Hall were taking part in another training exercise. It was not until the Volunteers occupied the General Post Office in O'Connell Street and several other large buildings in the heart of Dublin that anyone understood that it was a real rebellion. From the steps of the GPO, Pearse read out a proclamation establishing the Republic. On the roof flew two flags; the traditional green flag with a gold harp and the new Republican tricolour of green, white and orange.

For the rest of the week the Volunteers and Connolly's men, now the 'Army of the Irish Republic', held out against increasingly heavy infantry and artillery attack by British troops hurried from barracks in Ireland and shipped across the Irish Sea. By Saturday 29 April most

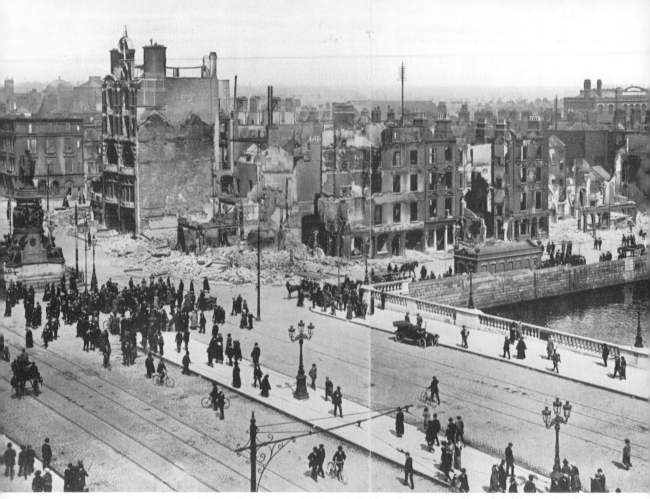

O'Connell Street near O'Connell Bridge, showing the effect of shelling during the rising.
The photograph comes from The Sphere, *13 May 1916*

of O'Connell Street lay in ruins and Pearse surrendered to General
Maxwell, who had been sent to take supreme command. The rebels
in Dublin, and in the few other scenes of fighting, were disarmed and
marched off to jail. The Easter Rising was over before anyone fully
understood what had happened.

It was estimated that only about 2000 rebel soldiers had been
involved. About 130 British soldiers and police, 60 rebels and around
250 civilians were killed. Damage to property came to about £2.5
million, mostly the result of the shelling of buildings in Dublin thought
to be occupied by rebel forces.

There was almost no popular support for the rising in Ireland. The
farmers were doing well out of the war. More food was being sold to
England as her overseas supplies were cut off. Horses were supplied
to the British Army. This all meant higher profits and more jobs.
Thousands of Irish families had menfolk serving in the Army and
sending home part of their pay to wives or parents. It was still taken
for granted that Home Rule would be given after the war and the
rising, if it had any effect, would only count against that.

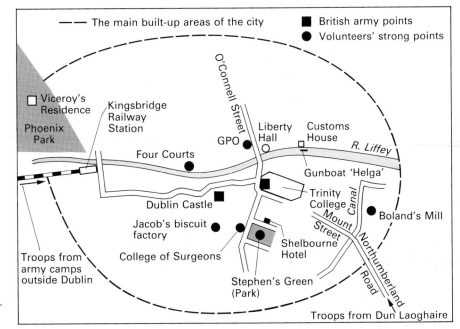

The main built-up areas of the city ■ British army points
● Volunteers' strong points

Dublin during the Easter Rising

Professional people and businessmen were particularly alarmed at the part played by the Citizen Army, which to them seemed to give the rising a hint of socialist revolution. This, and the pointless loss of life, led Catholic bishops, as well as Redmond and the nationalist MPs, to condemn the rising. The Protestant gentry, many of them now more or less accepting the prospect of Home Rule, were horrified at such an outbreak of anti-British violence. Ulster Unionists were in general less worried than amused at yet another ridiculous fiasco, similar to the rebellions of 1848 and 1867.

The aftermath of the rising

Asquith gave supreme civil and military authority in Ireland to General Maxwell. Maxwell could see only one way to deal with traitors and rebels who were in league with Germany. He set up courts-martial, and within four days of the surrender Tom Clarke, Patrick Pearse and Thomas MacDonagh were executed by firing squad on 3 May. From then up to 12 May another twelve leaders, including Connolly, were shot. (Roger Casement was later hanged on 3 August.) Seventy-five others were sentenced to death, and nearly 2000 people were sentenced to imprisonment or interned without trial.

The steadily mounting toll of executions from 3 May onwards began to turn public opinion in Ireland against Maxwell and the Government. The rebels had behaved as if they were the Irish Army, and the British troops were a foreign army of occupation. Some people felt that those who had surrendered should be treated as prisoners-of-war, rather than as traitors to be shot. The executions made it impossible for most Irish people to side with the British authorities against the men who were facing death for what they believed in. Redmond and the Home Rule MPs realised the effect the executions were having. Redmond's deputy, John Dillon, told the House of Commons

'You are letting loose a river of blood . . . between two races who, after three hundred years of hatred and of strife, we had nearly succeeded in bringing together.'

Asquith finally stopped the executions after 12 May, and handed the Irish problem over to David Lloyd George, who had made a name for himself as Minister of Munitions. Lloyd George was to have to cope with the problem for the next six years; from December 1916 onwards as Prime Minister. He first met Redmond and Carson, offering Home Rule with partition, but no agreement was reached. Later, in May 1917, he called an Irish Convention with members representing different views, but no new ideas resulted. Some people believed that Lloyd George was mainly anxious to convince people in Ireland, Britain, and the United States, that the Government was urgently trying to find a solution. From April 1917 the USA was Britain's valuable ally in the war and Americans, many of Irish descent, wanted to be sure that she was dealing fairly with Ireland.

The rise of Sinn Fein

The defeat of the Easter Rising was by no means the end of the IRB. It remained a secret society influencing events through its members in other organisations. The Volunteers also remained very active. An association and a fund were set up to keep relatives and friends of the imprisoned Volunteers in touch with each other and to provide money to help them.

Most of the Volunteers were kept at Frongoch Camp in North Wales, where they behaved as prisoners-of-war, not convicts. There was no sense of defeat, nor thought of giving up. De Valera, the most senior surviving officer, who had narrowly escaped execution in May, wrote from prison:

'The armed force started in 1913 must not be allowed to disappear. The Volunteers . . . must be kept as a permanent force at the country's back. That, it seems to us, is our mission as a body.'

By the end of 1916 all those who had been interned were released and returned to join their comrades who had been unable to take part in the rising. Although originally formed to support Home Rule, these Volunteers now began to support a more extreme nationalist party which was demanding complete independence.

The Sinn Fein Party had been started in 1905. Its founder, Arthur Griffith, wanted Ireland to be a separate, independent country, although he was originally prepared to accept Edward VII as King, but in name only. Sinn Fein did not have many members in 1916, but it was one of the loudest voices declaring that England's quarrel with Germany should not involve Ireland. Because the IRB was almost unknown, Sinn Fein got the blame (or credit) in the press for the Easter Rising, and Griffith was jailed, although he had not taken any part in it.

On Griffith's release from prison in December 1916 the Sinn Fein Party began to put forward candidates in by-elections. They gained three seats in 1917, defeating Home Rule candidates. Several other small nationalist groups merged with Sinn Fein in October 1917, and de Valera, one of the three Sinn Fein MPs, was elected President of the Party. As he was Commandant of the Volunteers he led both the political movement demanding independence, and the military organisation to support that demand.

Government policy 1917–18

The wartime government of Lloyd George was unable to spend much time thinking about Ireland in 1917. The only policy was simply to maintain law and order as they understood it. This meant arresting anyone found wearing Volunteer uniform or displaying the green, white and orange tricolour, breaking up parades and public meetings, and preventing any expression of anti-British feeling. Many Sinn Feiners were imprisoned and one Volunteer officer, Thomas Ashe, died while on hunger-strike in jail.

In April 1918 Parliament passed the Conscription Act, permitting men in Ireland to be drafted into the British Army. The rest of Britain had had conscription since 1916, but recruitment in Ireland had been voluntary. Now the Government was facing a desperate shortage of manpower, and the supply of recruits from Ireland had almost stopped since the Rising. Some British military men also recommended conscription as a way of knocking sense into Irish 'troublemakers'.

There was almost total opposition in Ireland to the threat of conscription. Sinn Fein naturally opposed it. The trade unions called a national strike in protest. The Catholic Church issued a strong statement upholding the right of the Irish people to resist it. The Home Rule MPs spoke out against it and walked out of the House of Commons in protest when they were ignored. The Government responded by appointing Field Marshal Lord John French as Viceroy of Ireland to impose something like martial law. Most of the Sinn Fein and Volunteer leaders were arrested and their organisations, as well as the Gaelic League, were declared illegal. The threat of conscription only ended in November 1918, with the end of the Great War.

The election of 1918

A general election was held in December, with all men over 21 and women over 30 voting for the first time. Lloyd George was re-elected at the head of a coalition of Liberals and Conservatives. In Ireland the Home Rule Party was reduced from sixty-eight to six seats, while the new Sinn Fein Party won seventy-three seats. In their election campaign Sinn Fein had promised to do three things if they were successful:

1. They would refuse to attend the House of Commons but would set up a separate assembly of elected representatives for Ireland.
2. They would appeal to the world statesmen, meeting at the Versailles Peace Conference, to recognise Ireland as an independent state.
3. They would resist any further attempt by the British authorities to rule Ireland.

Home Rule had always been a kind of half-independence, but the most that could reasonably be expected. Many more people now wanted, reasonably or not, to try for full independence, but several questions remained to be answered. Would Britain, reluctant to give Home Rule in the past, now allow Ireland to become a separate state? Would the Ulster Unionists, who had been ready to fight against Home Rule, now agree to become citizens of an independent Irish Republic? Would the Peace Conference of the victors in the Great War compel Britain to give the Irish freedom, as the Poles and the Czechs and other small nations were to be given freedom? At the end of 1918 most people would have answered 'No' to each question, but Sinn Fein MPs and their supporters were showing a spirit which had not been seen since the days of Parnell.

10

The War of Independence and the Treaty

De Valera and Collins

Two men stood out among the newly-elected Sinn Fein MPs. They were Eamon de Valera and Michael Collins. De Valera's father was a Spanish-American. He was born in 1882 and lived in New York up to the age of two. He was then brought to Ireland to live with his mother's family in County Limerick. He became a mathematics teacher, a Gaelic Leaguer, and one of the first recruits to the Irish Volunteers in 1913. In the Easter Rising he was in command of the Volunteers who occupied Boland's Mill, where some of the heaviest fighting took place. He was among the next batch of prisoners due to

De Valera speaking at an anti-conscription meeting at Ballaghadereen, County Roscommon, 1918

face the firing squad when Asquith stopped the executions on 12 May. His American birth may have affected Asquith's decision. Released in June 1917, he became leader of Sinn Fein and of the Volunteers. He was arrested in May 1918 on the orders of the new Viceroy, Lord French, and was still in jail when the post-war election was held in December, but he escaped soon after. Tall, thin and scholarly, de Valera was recommended by Griffith to the new Sinn Fein Party as 'A man in whom you will have a statesman as well as a soldier'.

Michael Collins, affectionately known as Mick, or the Big Fella, was born in County Cork in 1890. As a young man he worked as a clerk in London, but returned to Dublin early in 1916 and joined the Volunteers. He fought in the GPO during Easter Week and was interned with the other rank-and-file Volunteers. On his release he became one of the leading figures in the Republican movement through his enormous energy and cheerful friendliness. As Director of Organisation and Intelligence on the Volunteer staff, Collins built up a network of agents in the Irish Post Office, in the RIC and even among the Civil Servants in Dublin Castle. Daring, and at times ruthless towards enemies, Collins was the only leader to avoid arrest in May 1918. He kept the Republican movement going up to the election in December 1918.

The Sinn Fein Dail 1919

After winning the election the Sinn Fein MPs did not attend the Westminster parliament, but set themselves up in Dublin as Dail Eireann – the Assembly, or Parliament – of Ireland. They were no longer called MPs but TDs, which stood for Teachtai Dala – delegates of the Dail. Unionist and Home Rule MPs were invited to join in, but refused.

De Valera was elected President of the Dail. Other ministers were appointed for finance, justice, labour and so on, and they began to act, so far as they could, as if they were the real government of Ireland. Money was raised by selling Republican Bonds, since they could not collect taxes. They set up committees to make plans for future economic development, and established a system of courts. Many Sinn Fein candidates were successful in local government elections, and as a result some county councils acknowledged the Dail as the rightful governing authority in Ireland.

In the early days the Dail ministries and courts were laughed at, or simply ignored, but as time went on more people began to take them seriously. Even people employed by the British Government began to show signs of divided loyalty. The Chief Secretary for Ireland, Sir Hamar Greenwood, told the Cabinet in 1920

'We can only rely on the Navy, Military and RIC. The Dublin police cannot be relied on, nor the Post Office, nor the Civil Service.'

The Sinn Fein MPs had high hopes of the Peace Conference in Paris in 1919. Allied statesmen were setting up new states in Europe for

A Dail court hearing a case in Cork, 1920

peoples who had long been under foreign rule, such as the Poles and the Czechs. The Dail sent three TDs to Paris, but they were refused a hearing as Lloyd George declared that the question of Irish nationhood was an internal matter for the United Kingdom.

The Dail also expected diplomatic support, or even a recognition of the Irish Republic, from the US government, as well as money from Irish-American societies. This was so important that de Valera himself went to America in June 1919, where he remained until December 1920. He toured the country arousing a great deal of sympathy, but his efforts failed to persuade either the President or Congress to take up the cause of Irish independence. The US Government would not take sides against Britain, and most Americans, once the war was over, did not want to be involved in affairs in Europe.

The War of Independence 1919–21

The third part of Sinn Fein's policy, to resist British rule in Ireland, was intended to be a policy of passive resistance or civil disobedience. This meant ignoring the law and refusing to co-operate with the RIC and the courts. The Volunteers, now known as the Irish Republican Army, or IRA, had done no fighting since Easter 1916. Many young men in the IRA however felt like Dan Breen, who wrote later:

> 'We had had enough of being pushed around. . . . We considered that this business of getting in and out of jail was leading us nowhere.'

Breen was the leader of the first isolated attack on the RIC in January 1919, when two policemen were killed and a cartload of explosives was captured. The Church, the Dail, and even the IRA leaders disapproved of this action, and the British authorities continued to suppress newspapers, ban meetings and arrest speakers for the rest of the year without provoking any serious military reaction. Then, on 19 December 1919, the official car of the Viceroy, Lord John French, was attacked on the outskirts of Dublin and several of his bodyguard were wounded.

The attack was planned by Michael Collins and it marked the beginning of serious fighting in Ireland. The men who bore the brunt of the IRA offensive were the RIC. Up to this time, they had felt no great contradiction in being Irishmen in the service of the British government. Now the Dail was claiming their allegiance, and with IRA raids on their barracks increasing, they were doing less normal police work and more fighting. Many constables resigned from the RIC and few new recruits joined.

Lloyd George therefore authorised the recruitment of extra men in Britain. Most of them were ex-soldiers who knew how to handle guns and had not settled down to civilian life after the Great War. They were kitted out with a mixture of Army khaki and dark green RIC uniforms, with black belts and caps, and were soon nicknamed the Black-and-Tans. Later in 1920 another extra force was sent to Ireland, mainly ex-Army officers, officially called Police Cadets, but usually known as the Auxiliaries, or Auxies.

British troops and armed police numbered about 40,000. The IRA had about 15,000 members, but they were very short of guns, and Collins reckoned that only about 3000 IRA men were active at any one time. The main IRA attacks came in Dublin, Cork, and the south-western counties. The rest of Ireland was generally quiet.

In Belfast the IRA was on the defensive, attempting to protect Catholic families from attacks by Orange rioters which began in the summer of 1920. Crown Forces had the advantage in numbers, trans-

Black and Tans on patrol. The civilian hostages were supposed to discourage the IRA from attacking the truck

port and military equipment, but the IRA were fighting on home ground and made full use of ambush and surprise attack. They also had the support of the vast majority of the population. Many actively helped them; many more (except for a few of the old Protestant landlords) would at least not help the troops or police in any way. Black-and-Tan raids and searches for arms or wanted men did nothing to make the civilian population more loyal to the British Crown.

IRA action generally took the form of attacks on police barracks and ambushes of small patrols or convoys of lorries. Roads were blocked by trenches or felled trees, and sometimes an attack on a small British unit was followed by the planned ambush of a larger force coming to the rescue. One of the most successful local IRA leaders was Tom Barry, commander of the West Cork Flying Column. He had served in the British Army from 1915 to 1919.

The Black-and-Tans' main object was to capture wanted members of Sinn Fein and the IRA. As they often failed, frustration led them to shoot-up the village where they thought their quarry was hiding, roaring through in their specially adapted lorries, Crossley Tenders, firing indiscriminately. The Co-operative Creameries run by dairy farmers were often bombed or burnt in order to punish a community for failing to help in the capture of an IRA man. Early in 1921 such general reprisals were officially authorised, and selected houses in the vicinity of any IRA attack were blown up. The IRA responded by burning down the big country houses of Protestant landlords.

In the autumn and winter of 1920 the fighting became fiercer and hatred more bitter. Lloyd George's government was smarting from sharp criticism, abroad and in Britain, over its dealing with Ireland. The military authorities were still unable to defeat the IRA. At the same time, Collins knew that he could not keep up the struggle for ever. The IRA were constantly losing men in action, and civilian Sinn Fein leaders were being arrested and jailed in large numbers. Both sides desperately needed to win soon.

On 21 November 1920 eleven British secret agents were shot in their homes in Dublin by Collins's 'execution squad'. As he said later, 'I found out that those fellows we put on the spot were going to put a lot of us on the spot, so I got in first'. In the afternoon of the same day Black-and-Tans opened fire on the crowd at a Gaelic football match in Croke Park, Dublin, killing twelve spectators and wounding sixty. Later that evening three IRA suspects in custody in Dublin were 'shot while attempting to escape'. Soon after this 'Bloody Sunday', General Crozier, the Auxiliaries' commander, resigned, saying that his men's discipline had completely broken down.

On 28 November Tom Barry's West Cork Flying Column completely wiped out a convoy of eighteen Auxiliaries. A fortnight later Auxiliaries and Black-and-Tans started fires in Cork which burnt down most of the centre of the city. In May 1921 the IRA struck in Dublin itself, where they captured and burned down the Customs House.

These events stood out amongst a constant succession of minor raids, ambushes, reprisals and counter-reprisals. Not a day passed without newspaper reports of arrests, escapes, shooting incidents and murders. A curfew was imposed in many places. Military courts held trials without juries, and, some people believed, without evidence. What attracted most sympathetic attention in Britain and abroad were the hunger-strikes by prisoners who refused to accept that British courts had any right to try them. The most notable hunger-striker was Terence MacSwiney, Lord Mayor of Cork, who died on 25 October 1920 after seventy-four days without food.

The effects of the fighting

As well as the actual loss of life, the fighting damaged the Irish economy. Trade and transport were hampered, firms closed down, and jobs were lost. In places the authorities banned markets and fairs. More visible signs of the war appeared every week: burnt-out police barracks, houses in ruins, wrecked creameries, demolished bridges.

Lloyd George's policy, and particuarly the activities of the Black-and-Tans, turned many moderate nationalists against Britain. His policy was also criticised in Britain itself, and in the Commonwealth. Lloyd George's view was that the troubles in Ireland were the fault of a small number of extremists, and in 1920 he proudly announced 'We have murder by the throat'. His critics knew, however, that Sinn Fein stood for what most Irish people wanted, and that sooner or later he would have to talk to their leaders to reach a settlement.

Partition and Treaty negotiations

Lloyd George had, in fact, already decided how to settle the question in his own way. This was to grant Home Rule at last, but with Partition. In December 1919 he introduced in the Commons a Bill for the Better Government of Ireland. It was passed in 1920 and came into force in May 1921. This Government of Ireland Act divided Ireland into two parts: Northern Ireland and Southern Ireland. Northern Ireland was made up of six Ulster counties: Antrim, Down, Armagh, Londonderry, Tyrone and Fermanagh. Southern Ireland consisted of the other twenty-six counties.

Northern Ireland comprised only these six counties instead of the nine counties of the historic Province of Ulster, because the three which were excluded (Donegal, Cavan and Monaghan) had a population of 260,000 Catholics, presumed to be nationalists, and only 70,000 Prot-estants. If all nine counties were included it was feared that Unionists in Northern Ireland might not always be in a majority.

The two parts of Ireland were each to have its own Home Rule Parliament, subject to the United Kingdom Parliament at West-minster. The separate elections to the Southern Ireland and the Northern Ireland Parliaments took place in May 1921. In the South Sinn Fein did not accept Lloyd George's decision, but merely made

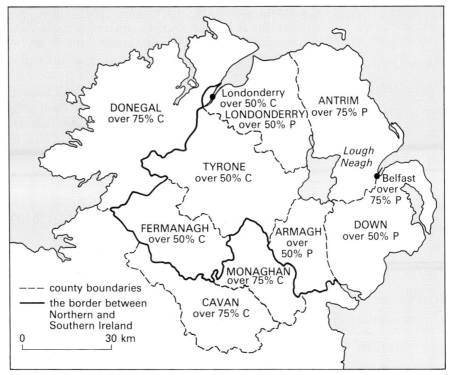

The nine counties of Ulster in the census of 1911. When Northern Ireland was created, three counties with large Catholic majorities were left out, but two with smaller Catholic majorities were included

use of the official voting arrangements to elect a new Dail. In the North the Unionists won forty seats out of fifty-two. The Northern Ireland Parliament was opened by George V on 22 June 1921. James Craig, the Northern Ireland Prime Minister, made it clear that in his view the future of the Six Counties was settled for good.

As Sinn Fein had ignored his Government of Ireland Act, Lloyd George decided that he would have to talk to them. On 25 June he invited de Valera to London. General Macready, the British Commander-in-Chief, agreed on a truce with the IRA on 11 July, and on the following day de Valera arrived in London. After discussions a full conference was arranged to begin early in October. De Valera decided that, as President of the Dail, he should stay in Ireland, so the Irish Delegation was led by Arthur Griffith and Michael Collins.

In the negotiations several matters were agreed fairly easily. Trade relations were settled and the Royal Navy was to retain three naval bases in Southern Ireland. The more important question of status caused long argument. The Irish delegates wanted independence, whereas Lloyd George was determined to keep some British control over Ireland, and would not consider recognising an independent Republic. The most he would offer was that the twenty-six county area should be known as the Irish Free State, and should be a Dominion of the British Commonwealth, with self-government similar to that of

Canada. They also discussed the position of Northern Ireland, already established by the Government of Ireland Act. Lloyd George would not alter this, but he promised Griffith and Collins that he would appoint a Boundary Commission, to re-draw the border between North and South. This, he suggested, would transfer districts where there was a majority of Catholics and Nationalists from the Six Counties to the Free State. He insisted though, that Southern Ireland must remain within the British Commonwealth and that Irish TDs must take an oath of allegiance to the Crown. In the end, in the early hours of 6 December 1921, with Lloyd George threatening to break off the talks and resume full-scale war, the Irish delegates signed the Treaty.

The Creation of the Irish Free State

Most people in Britain were very pleased that Lloyd George had solved the 'Irish problem' at last. The *Manchester Guardian* congratulated him on 'a splendid achievement', and *The Times* looked forward to 'a new era of happiness and mutual understanding'.

In Southern Ireland, however, there was a general feeling that the Treaty was a second-best agreement. Collins defended it on the grounds that it gave Ireland 'the freedom to achieve freedom', but de Valera issued a statement refusing to accept the terms which were 'in violent conflict with the wishes of the majority of this nation'.

The Dail met on 14 December and continued to debate whether to accept or reject the Treaty until 7 January 1922. Those TDs who followed Griffith and Collins believed that they had got the best bargain possible at that time. The TDs who agreed with de Valera could not accept that Ireland as a member of the British Commonwealth would have to recognise the British Crown. They wanted nothing less than complete independence. One TD, Liam Mellows, expressed this feeling with the words:

> 'To my mind, the Republic does exist. It is . . . something for which men gave their lives, for which men were hanged. . . . There was no question of making a bargain over this thing, over the honour of Ireland, because I hold that the honour of Ireland is too sacred a thing to make a bargain over.'

When the vote was taken at the end of the debates in the Dail, sixty-four TDs voted to ratify the Treaty but fifty-seven were against it. De Valera resigned as President of the Dail and was replaced by Arthur Griffith. Michael Collins became head of the new Irish Free State Government. He and Griffith and the pro-Treaty TDs began to take over from the British authorities. British troops and the Black-and-Tans and Auxiliaries started to leave Ireland. The RIC was disbanded and was replaced by a new police force, the Garda Siochana (Civic Guards), and the IRA began to be formed into the Free State Army.

The newest member of the Commonwealth, the Irish Free State of Twenty-Six Counties, was launched.

11

The Irish Free State and Eire to 1945

The Irish Civil War

The Irish Free State was in existence only a few months when fighting began between the pro-Treaty and anti-Treaty groups. Both Collins and de Valera tried hard to avoid this, but no compromise was possible. The IRA was not a professional army, but an army of volunteers with strong political feelings. Many local commanders, especially in the south-west, came out against the Treaty, and, in alliance with de Valera and his section of the Sinn Fein party, became known as the Irregulars, or Republicans. The men who accepted the Treaty and the authority of Collins formed the new Free State army, the Free Staters.

In April 1922 the Irregulars occupied the Four Courts building in Dublin, one of the Volunteer strongholds in 1916. Collins took no action against them until June, when they took hostage J. J. 'Ginger' O'Connell, a senior Free State Army General. Collins then, on 28 June, attacked the Four Courts, using field artillery borrowed from the British troops who had not yet left Dublin. This sparked off widespread fighting in the country between Republicans and Free Staters.

The Irregulars' commander was Liam Lynch, who announced 'We have declared for an Irish Republic and will not live under any other law'. Within a month he was compelled to withdraw behind a line roughly from Limerick to Waterford, the 'Munster Republic'. The Free Staters got control of Cork city by sending in shiploads of troops, and the fighting soon became a guerilla war of raids and ambushes similar to the war against the British in 1920–1.

During the course of the fighting in August 1922, Michael Collins was killed in an ambush in County Cork. He was thirty-three. Arthur Griffith also died in August from a stroke brought on by overwork. They were replaced by William Cosgrave and Kevin O'Higgins, who increased army and police pressure on the Irregulars and their supporters. Special military courts were set up, suspects were imprisoned without trial, and the death penalty was imposed for possession of unauthorised guns. Several leaders and many men on both sides

Free State troops being shipped to Cork, August 1922. Notice the gun labelled
'FOUR COURTS'

were assassinated or executed by firing squad on the orders of those
who had been comrades-in-arms only a year before, and the bitterness
increased month by month.

In April 1923 Liam Lynch was killed in action and the Irregulars
finally realised that their cause was hopeless. The Church condemned
them, and most people supported the Free State Government. The
IRA leaders discussed the situation with de Valera, who knew that
people were weary of the fighting. Members of the IRA were therefore
ordered on 24 May 1923 to return to their homes and conceal their
guns. No agreement was made between the Free State Government
and the Republicans; there were no terms of surrender and no
amnesty. The police continued to hunt down wanted men and the
Republicans made it clear that they still felt free to try to overthrow
the Free State whenever they had the chance.

Steps towards freedom

The Treaty which Griffith and Collins signed stated that the Free State
was a Dominion of the British Commonwealth, with the same status
as Canada, and this definition was repeated in the Free State constitution. Collins, and after his death, Kevin O'Higgins, took the view

that the exact meaning of 'Dominion' could be changed in time. Three important marks of Dominion status in 1922 were:

1. The elected representatives of the people had to take an oath of allegiance to the British Crown.
2. The Crown was represented by a Governor-General.
3. Appeals in certain legal cases could be taken to the Privy Council in London.

From the start, the Free State Government tried to defy the limits placed on Dominion countries. Cosgrave made the Free State a member of the League of Nations and he sent ambassadors to countries outside the Commonwealth, including one to the USA in 1924. These moves to show the Free State's determination to act as one of the world's independent countries were often supported by other Dominions, especially Canada and South Africa. Their annoyance at the limitations on Dominions came to a head at the Commonwealth Conference in 1926. Members signed a declaration that Britain and the Dominions were each equal in status and no member of the Commonwealth was superior to any other. The British Parliament accepted this when it passed the Statute of Westminster in 1931. From then on, it seemed clear that a Dominion could leave the Commonwealth whether Britain agreed or not.

Cosgrave's government fell in 1932 and his successor, de Valera, wasted no time in removing the remnants of British rule. First the oath of allegiance was abolished by the Dail in 1933, then the position of Governor-General, and then the right of appeal to the Privy Council. In 1935 the Privy Council itself ruled that the Dail had the authority to do this.

While Britain was concerned with the abdication of Edward VIII in 1936 de Valera passed the External Relations Act, which completely abolished the authority of the Crown in the Irish Free State, but recognised the King as Head of the Commonwealth. The Free State was no longer 'a member of' but merely 'associated with' the British Commonwealth, and the King was authorised to act on its behalf in diplomatic relations with other countries. This idea of 'external association' had been put forward by de Valera during the Treaty negotiations in 1921, but no one really understood it at that time.

The change in status was underlined by the new constitution of Ireland introduced by de Valera in 1937. The term Irish Free State was dropped and, although the word Republic was not used in the constitution, the Head of State was to be an elected President. The constitution was designed to apply to the whole of Ireland, though it was limited to the Twenty-Six Counties until such time as the North would be reunited with the South. In the Gaelic text of the constitution, the Gaelic word Eire, meaning Ireland, was used. The British press began to use Eire as a convenient name for the twenty-six-county area only, although the word really meant the whole island.

British Governments protested at each step which Cosgrave and de Valera took, but they made no attempts to retaliate. Even in 1937, with a President as Head of State, Britain and other countries continued to act as if Eire was a member of the Commonwealth. Political relations were so good in 1938 that the three Treaty naval bases were handed back to Irish control. Irish people who went to work in Britain were treated as if they were British citizens, and there were no restrictions on travel between the two countries. Although Eire's independence was clearly shown by her neutrality during the Second World War, large numbers of Irish men and women worked in Britain and served in the British Forces.

After the war, in 1949, a government of Fine Gael and the small parties came to power. This Inter-Party Government separated Eire completely from the Commonwealth and set up the Republic of Ireland. A completely independent republic was achieved at last, but only for the Twenty-Six Counties. A cynical jingle of the time echoed the words of earlier patriotic songs:

> 'God save the Southern Part of Ireland!
> Three-quarters of a nation once again.'

The British Government agreed that the kind of dual citizenship which existed should continue, even though the Republic could no longer be regarded as a Commonwealth country. At the same time Britain gave a firm assurance that the position of Northern Ireland would never be changed without the consent of its parliament.

The gun in politics

The end of the Civil War in May 1923 did not mean the end of attempts to uphold Republicanism by force of arms. Having fought against British forces during the War of Independence (see pages 53–6) and against the Free State Army and Garda during the Civil War, many of the IRA felt it was their duty to continue to wage war until the all-Ireland Republic became a reality.

Cosgrave's Free State Government was determined to suppress them. Public Safety Acts in 1923, 1924 and 1926 imposed very severe penalties for offences such as armed robbery and illegal possession of fire-arms. At first de Valera and the anti-Treaty TDs kept up the claim to be the true Republican government and were nominally in control of the IRA. In 1926, however, de Valera separated from the Republican Sinn Fein and set up his own party, Fianna Fail. Fianna Fail members were willing to take their seats in the Dail, if they could avoid taking the oath of allegiance to the Crown. Determined Republicans kept the name of Sinn Fein; Cosgrave's supporters meanwhile had formed the Cumann na nGaedheal party. In 1927 de Valera and the Fianna Fail TDs were finally admitted to the Dail, having signed the register (though they persisted in the view that this did not mean they had taken the oath).

IRA shootings and attacks on Garda barracks continued throughout 1926 and 1927, and in July 1927, Kevin O'Higgins, Cosgrave's Home

Affairs minister, the 'strong man' of the Government, was assassinated. Cosgrave passed another Public Safety Act in 1931, under which suspects could be tried by a Military Tribunal, as juries were often afraid to convict captured gunmen. The IRA was also declared an illegal organisation. De Valera and the Fianna Fail TDs, who now formed the normal opposition in the Dail, protested at the Government's campaign against the IRA. There were many personal links between Fianna Fail and the IRA.

Cumann na nGaedheal lost the general election in 1932, and so de Valera now headed the Government. Fianna Fail ministers took up office with revolvers in their pockets, it is said, fearing that their old Civil War enemies would attempt a massacre. They immediately released the IRA men who had been imprisoned, and abolished the Military Tribunal. The Republicans expected de Valera to sack large numbers of officials, judges, and Free State Army officers, who had served under Cosgrave, but he did not. Republicans, however, took to breaking up political meetings of Cumann na nGaedheal. Cumann na nGaedheal joined with a Free State Army ex-officers' association to form a new party, Fine Gael, and a uniformed group, the Blueshirts, was recruited in 1933 to protect Fine Gael leaders and public meetings. Many people feared that the Blueshirts and their leader, Eoin O'Duffy, would try to establish a dictatorship in Ireland, but the movement soon died out.

Under de Valera's rule the IRA were no more law-abiding, as he did not create the Republic as fast as they would have liked, although he quickly abolished the hated oath of allegiance and other marks of Dominion status. De Valera soon found that, as head of an elected government, he could not tolerate an armed organisation which behaved as a law unto itself. One instance of this was their 'execution' in March 1936 of the retired Admiral Somerville, whose offence was to write character references for young men of his neighbourhood who wanted to join the Royal Navy. In June 1936, de Valera's Government declared the IRA illegal.

De Valera hoped that the Republicans would accept the New Constitution which he issued in 1937, since it created a republic in all but name, and claimed to apply to the whole of Ireland. A few leading IRA members, notably Sean MacBride, were satisfied, but the majority were not, and their military action continued, in the form of attacks on customs posts along the Northern Ireland Border.

Early in 1939 the IRA began a series of bomb attacks in England, having first sent a declaration of war to the British Foreign Secretary. They intended to disrupt communications and business life to such an extent that Britain would agree to discuss their grievances. Civilian injuries were inevitable, with explosions in pillar-boxes, stations, and other public buildings. The most serious incident took place in Coventry on 25 August when a bomb killed five people and injured seventy. De Valera was angered by such outrages, knowing the effect they would have on British public opinion at a time when he was anxious to keep Southern Ireland neutral in the coming European war.

His Government passed the Offences against the State Act in 1939 which restored the Military Tribunal and internment without trial.

During the Second World War supplies of money for the IRA from America were cut off and IRA leaders in Dublin were harassed by Garda Special Branch detectives. Some were killed in gun-battles, some died on hunger-strike, many were simply locked up.

Distrust, and suspicion of an informer at the top of the organisation, added to their difficulties, and by the end of the war in 1945 the IRA was regarded as totally broken, without leaders and without funds.

The Border and the North

In the Treaty of 1921 it was agreed that a Boundary Commission would be set up to re-draw the Border between Northern Ireland and the Free State. Lloyd George gave the Irish delegates the impression that large areas would be transferred to the Free State. They hoped that Northern Ireland, with a much smaller area and population, would not be able to function, and the Unionists would soon make a bargain to re-unite with the Free State.

The Boundary Commission began its work in 1924. Eoin MacNeill represented the Free State. The Northern Ireland Prime Minister, James Craig, refused to appoint a representative, so Britain appointed one for him, and chose a South African judge as a neutral chairman. The three Commissioners had spent almost a year studying the border problem, when a newspaper, the *Morning Post*, claimed to have information that the Commission was going to recommend only very small adjustments to the Border. MacNeill resigned, and a hurried meeting was arranged, in October 1925, between Craig, Cosgrave and Stanley Baldwin, the British Prime Minister. To prevent riots and bloodshed they agreed that the Commissioners' Report should be kept secret and the Border should be left as it was. This outcome was a great disappointment to people in the Free State and to Nationalists in Northern Ireland.

A Council of Ireland to encourage co-operation, which might lead to eventual unity, had also been proposed in the Treaty, but this idea was not taken up. Unionist politicians turned their backs on the whole idea of re-unification. British Governments looked on it as something for the North and South to settle on their own. Leaders in Southern Ireland persisted in the view that, as Britain had established Partition, she should end it by putting pressure on Unionist leaders. These politicians in Southern Ireland, like Parnell and Redmond earlier, greatly underestimated the determination of ordinary Protestants in the North to remain British. They mistakenly believed that the only real opposition to re-unification came from Unionist Party leaders and big businessmen.

De Valera frequently referred to the 'injustice' of Partition, and was embarrassed that the IRA could claim to be fighting to abolish the Border while the elected Government of the Free State was making no progress. His removal of traces of British control between 1933 and 1938, however, made any chance of re-unification even less likely. The statement in the 1937 Constitution that the Dublin Government claimed the right to rule 'the whole island of Ireland' antagonised Northern Unionists greatly, even though 'association with' the Commonwealth was meant to reassure those who wanted to retain a connection with Britain.

Although he agreed to hand back the Treaty Ports in 1938, the British Prime Minister, Neville Chamberlain, would not put pressure on Northern Ireland to accept re-unification. In turn de Valera refused to make a military pact with Britain so long as the Border remained. In 1939 he warned that this was also the reason for the IRA bombing campaign. During the Second World War de Valera protested at the establishment of US bases in Northern Ireland, and resisted American pressure to join the Allies, again giving the Partition of Ireland as a reason.

By the end of the war in 1945 the ending of Partition was further away than ever. The Government and people of Northern Ireland had helped the Allied war effort in many ways, and had shared in the sufferings of mainland Britain from German bombs, rationing, and other discomforts. Eire had remained at best a friendly neutral. It was unthinkable that a British Government would 'hand over' the North, or that the North would allow itself to be handed over.

Land, industry and trade

One of the oldest arguments in favour of Irish self-government was that it would result in economic progress, but after the Treaty the state of the economy did not change. The Irish Free State had few mineral or fuel resources, and little industry. England was still the nearest and best market for agricultural produce and the most convenient supplier of manufactured goods and non-European commodities such as tea and tobacco. Cosgrave's Government followed a policy of keeping taxation and state spending down, leaving business to businessmen, and not imposing import duties on goods from abroad. Ireland was also affected by the general fall in prices of farm produce after 1920 and by the world depression in the 1930s.

The various Land Acts under British rule had begun to turn tenant farmers into farm owners. After independence this process was completed. The state provided the money to buy out the landlord, and the farmer repaid the state in instalments. Farms generally remained small and farming methods were backward. The Department of Agriculture attempted to improve the quality of produce, and the state-financed Agricultural Credit Corporation lent money to modernise farms. However, Irish farmers were very cautious and the amounts borrowed were generally less than £100. There was no increase in the amount of wasteland taken into cultivation, and the emphasis on cattle rather than crop-growing continued.

The economic war 1932–8

After the establishment of the Free State farmers who had bought their farms before 1922 continued to repay the money which the British Government had lent. These Land Annuities were now paid to the Free State Government which transferred the money to Britain. In 1932 de Valera stopped paying the Land Annuities to Britain, though he still collected the money from the farmers. Britain retaliated by putting a 20 per cent import duty on Irish goods, which hit the cattle trade very hard. This began the so-called economic war which lasted until 1938.

The Fianna Fail Government tried to make Irish farmers less dependent on the British market. They encouraged them to cut down on cattle and increase crops such as sugar-beet and wheat, which were not well suited to the Irish climate. In 1932 de Valera greatly increased import duties on goods, including coal, which mostly came from Britain. He hoped that making British goods dearer would encourage Irish businessmen to set up factories to produce the same commodities. The long-term aim was that Ireland should grow or make everything the Irish people could need. Sean Lemass, de Valera's right-hand man, said 'We believe that Ireland can be made a self-contained unit'.

As in most economic wars, both sides suffered. The Free State did achieve some economic development but Irish people wanted British goods and coal as much as the English wanted their beef and dairy produce. The two Governments recognised this in 1935, when they made a Coal-Cattle Pact which increased the trade in these two commodities. In 1938 they made a general trade agreement which brought the economic war to an end. Just a year later the Second World War broke out and the Free State had to redouble its efforts to become self-sufficient, now that it became almost impossible to import sugar, wheat, coal and other goods.

State enterprise

One feature of the Free State economy between 1921 and 1945 was important and unusual. Large-scale economic developments required large amounts of capital, but it was impossible to raise enough money in the Free State or to attract investments from abroad. Profits were not likely to be high enough or come quickly enough. The only body which could provide sufficient money, and could afford to wait a long time to recover it, was the State itself.

The first major state enterprise was the Shannon Scheme, begun in 1929. A hydro-electric generating station was built at Ardnacrusha, near Limerick, and an Electricity Supply Board was set up to distribute the current. Every town and most villages had electricity by 1943. Similar State-regulated bodies were Milk Boards; the Irish Hospitals Trust; Bord Failte, the Tourist Board; and Aer Lingus. During the Second World War the Irish Shipping Company was

THE FIRST NON-TARIFF COW.

" With the tariff off, she can afford to travel in comfort !''

British duties on Irish cattle were removed in 1938 as part of the trade agreement. This cartoon was printed in Dublin Opinion, *June 1938*

created by the State in an effort to keep overseas trade flowing. After the war CIE, the national transport authority, and Bord na Mona, the Turf (peat) Board, followed.

Such state-controlled industries did not result from any socialist theories about nationalisation. During the 1920s and 1930s socialist ideas, common in Britain and Europe, did not exist in Ireland. National politics were concerned with status, relations with Britain, and Partition. Devout Catholics, still the majority in the Free State, assumed that socialism was akin to communism, and therefore godless. Socialism did not appeal to farmers, and since industries remained small and trade unions were weak, there was no large organised working class to support it.

Gaelic nationalism

The founders of the Gaelic League in 1893 had seen the Irish language as vital to the revival of a distinct Irish culture. Most politically-minded people took it for granted that there would be a real recovery of Gaelic under the Free State Government. Official forms and notices were printed in both Irish and English and the wording on the new Irish stamps and coins was in Irish. State employees, including the Army, the Garda, and Post Office workers, had to know Irish and some correspondence between government departments was carried on exclusively in Irish. In general, however, there were no political or economic disadvantages for the vast majority of adults who could not speak or write in Irish.

Primary and secondary schools were required to teach Irish, and were encouraged to use the language in teaching other subjects. Extra grants were made to purchase Irish text-books, and higher salaries were paid to teachers who were fluent Gaelic speakers. In spite of state encouragement and the work of the Gaelic League and other language societies, the schools did not produce a new generation of Irish speakers. Parents explained, rather shamefaced, that their children found it difficult to learn, that it would be no use to them in getting a job, and that a better knowledge of English and other school subjects was more important. Most people did not feel any less Irish for not using the Gaelic language, although they did still feel a reverence for it, and an admiration for anyone who was a real Gaelic scholar and could speak the language fluently.

Another method of reviving the Irish language was to give special help to the few small districts where everybody still spoke Gaelic. These were known as the Gaeltacht and were mostly in the extreme west of Ireland. As this was also the least fertile part of Ireland, young people continued to emigrate from there, and the Gaelic-speaking population continued to decline.

English influence through books and magazines, which nationalists had deplored in the late nineteenth century, continued after 1921. English and American ideas, attitudes, and fashions now also began to spread through the radio and films. To counteract these, film censorship began in 1925 and a Censorship Board was set up for magazines and books in 1926. Most people accepted this as necessary. It was rather inconsistent, however, that Irish authors such as James Joyce could be recognised as worldwide leaders in modern literature and yet have their books banned in Ireland. The national broadcasting service, Radio Eireann, was started in 1926, and contributed to the

THE DESERTED VILLAGE.

Emigration to Britain continued throughout the 1930s; a picture from Dublin Opinion, *January 1937*

encouragement of the language with some programmes in Irish, but this did not prevent large numbers of people from listening to BBC broadcasts from London.

One popular feature of the nineteenth-century Gaelic Revival which continued was Gaelic football and hurling. These remained majority player and spectator sports in the Free State, far more widely supported than association football, rugby or cricket. Irish singing and Irish dancing survived, but most young people were also keen to listen to modern dance music on English records or the BBC and to try the dances they saw in Hollywood films.

Religion

The Catholic Church remained supreme in the Free State, though both the clergy themselves and the Free State Government resisted calls by Catholic extremists to root out Protestantism. The State took trouble to show that there was no religious discrimination against the Church of Ireland or other Protestant Churches. De Valera chose the Protestant founder of the Gaelic League, Dr Douglas Hyde, to be the first President of Eire under the 1937 Constitution, and the Catholic Church was given special recognition only as the religion of the majority.

The Catholic Church did tend to dictate to its own members, forbidding the children of mixed marriages to be brought up as Protestants and forbidding Catholic students to attend Trinity College, Dublin, which was still regarded as a Protestant University. Catholic influence was also shown in the ban on the sale of contraceptives, the fact that divorce was not recognised by law, and the practical impossibility of obtaining legal abortion. At that time, of course, such matters were also much less commonplace in Britain and America.

Various Catholic organisations played a very large part in social welfare. The Irish Free State was relatively poor and state pensions, unemployment and sickness benefits were either non-existent or very small. The teaching orders of the Catholic Church continued to supply very large numbers of the staff in schools. The parish priest still acted as a community leader, especially in country parishes, sometimes dominating his flock in a way which would not have been attempted in other Catholic countries in Europe.

The obvious Gaelicism and Catholicism of the Free State and Eire, as well as the gradual removal of any remaining ties with Britain, made Ulster Unionists less likely than ever to consider throwing in their lot with the South.

12
Northern Ireland 1920-45

Establishing Unionist control

The sub-state of Northern Ireland was established by Lloyd George's Government of Ireland Act 1920. This Act was to set up a form of Home Rule in the two parts of Ireland, but the South became a British Dominion by the Treaty of December 1921. The first Parliament of the Six Counties had already been opened in Belfast in June 1921. It had limited authority, no control over defence, trade, nor most taxation. Any laws it made could be overruled by the Westminster Parliament in which Northern Ireland was represented by twelve MPs elected separately.

The first Belfast Parliament contained forty Unionist MPs out of a total of fifty-two. Many Unionists would have preferred the Six Counties to remain simply as a part of the United Kingdom, without a separate parliament, but they quickly accepted the limited self-government they were given. James Craig, the first Prime Minister, saw the advantages and would not even consider any further change. He ignored the Treaty talks, and refused to take part in the Boundary Commission, using the slogan, 'What we have, we hold'; and referred to the possibility of some Six-County land being transferred to the Free State with the words 'Not an inch'.

Unionist politicians liked to talk about 'Protestant Ulster' but even with 'Ulster' reduced to six counties, about one-third of the population were Catholics, most of whom wanted to go in with the rest of Ireland. The other two-thirds were Presbyterians or members of the Church of Ireland, the vast majority of whom wished to remain in the United Kingdom.

Since the First Home Rule Bill in 1886 there had been outbreaks of fighting between Nationalists and Unionists, and in the early days of Northern Ireland rioting was frequent and serious. In Belfast in November 1921 twenty-six people were killed, many injured and widespread damage caused. In the spring of 1922, Nationalists were refusing to recognise the Government's authority and some Nationalist

British troops keeping peace in Londonderry in July 1920

local councils declared their allegiance to the Free State. The IRA attacked the police and tried to get control over Catholic-populated areas north of the border. There were hopes, or fears, that the new sub-state of Northern Ireland would collapse in chaos.

Craig, as Prime Minister, was determined that this should not happen. When the Royal Ulster Constabulary replaced the RIC, an extra force of part-time Special Constables was raised, the B Specials. Both they and the regular RUC were issued with guns. The Special Powers Act was passed which gave the Northern Ireland Home Secretary unlimited authority to arrest and detain anyone, confiscate any property, impose a curfew, ban meetings or take any other steps necessary to preserve the peace. One MP said that the Special Powers Act could be reduced to a single statement, 'The Home Secretary shall have power to do what he likes, or else let somebody else do what he likes for him'.

In May 1922 armed police swept up 500 members of the IRA and Republican sympathisers who were interned without trial, and an 11 p.m. curfew was imposed over the whole of Northern Ireland. When the Civil War began in the Free State in the summer of 1922, IRA attacks came to an end in the North, and the danger that Craig and the Unionists would lose control over the Six Counties was over. The new parliament building at Stormont outside Belfast, opened in 1932, was meant to be a symbol that their control would last for ever.

The economy of Northern Ireland

Unionist leaders hoped that the link with Britain would bring prosperity and this would lead the majority of Catholics to accept their unwanted British citizenship. Prosperity, however, failed to arrive in the 1920s and 1930s. This failure did not come about from the division of Ireland, although the need to maintain customs posts along the border was a waste of money for both Irish states. The small farmers of Northern Ireland continued along the same lines as their counterparts in the Free State. Livestock rearing for export to Britain was their main occupation, and the Government encouraged more modern methods of farming. Cattle farmers benefited from the high British duties on Free State cattle during the economic war in the 1930s.

Northern Ireland's prosperity depended mainly, however, on the health of its industries, centred on Belfast (63 per cent of the population lived within a 50 kilometre radius of the centre of Belfast) and to a much smaller extent on Londonderry. These industries suffered a long-term decline, made worse by the effects of the Great War of 1914-18 on the staple British industries and the general depression in world trade in the 1930s. The linen industry was affected by competition from cotton and rayon. Shipbuilding met the same fate as shipbuilding elsewhere in Britain. In 1933 no ships were launched at Harland and Wolff's yard, and in 1934 Workman and Clark closed down. Connected industries such as engineering were also hit. No new factories were opened, like those making motor vehicles and electrical goods which gave new prosperity to the Midlands and the South of England. In the 1920s unemployment averaged 15 per cent; in the 1930s it averaged about 25 per cent. In common with governments elsewhere at the time, the Government of Northern Ireland was reluctant to become directly involved in industry and trade, and unwilling to borrow money to establish new industries. Lack of money was also a reason for failing to improve housing, public health and social welfare.

This kind of situation might have led to complaints from trade unions on behalf of the unemployed and perhaps a change of government. There were complaints, but at each election the Unionist Party won, with a large majority. Craig was Prime Minister until he died in 1940, and Unionist MPs generally retained their seats in Parliament until they retired or died. The trade unions were split between those which were linked to the British trade union movement, and those which looked to Dublin. The Labour Party got little support from Catholic workers, whose Church warned them of the evils of socialism. Protestant workers were warned that unless they voted Unionist they were in danger of being 'handed over' to a Catholic government in Dublin, and that seemed a worse fate than unemployment, poverty and ill-health.

Briefly, in 1932, unemployed Protestants and Catholics demonstrated together against the reduction in their dole money, but unemployment usually only increased competition for jobs and mutual.

hatred. In July 1935 the police had to build barricades between Catholic and Protestant areas of Belfast. Rioting led to 11 deaths, nearly 600 injuries, and over 500 cases of arson and damage to property.

The Nationalist minority

The Six Counties had been selected in order to give Northern Ireland the biggest possible area in which there would be a very large majority of Protestant Unionists over Catholic Nationalists. One result of this was that the Unionist Government was faced with a one-third minority of people who were mostly unwilling to help and often actively disloyal. Because of this, and the long-standing ill-will between Protestants and Catholics, the Unionist Party made great efforts to ensure that the Nationalist minority should have as little influence as possible. The Government of Ireland Act had laid down that parliamentary elections should be by the proportional representation system to make sure that the minority could elect some MPs. In 1929 the Unionist government abolished this system of voting.

Several schemes were used to keep Unionist control over local districts where there was a Catholic majority, or near-majority. First, the right to vote in local elections was limited to householders and property owners. This was also then the case in Britain and in the Irish Free State, but in Northern Ireland it meant that many Catholics, being generally poorer, had no vote in local elections. Secondly, proportional representation was abolished in local elections as early as 1922, which meant that Labour Party or Independent candidates stood very little chance of winning seats on local councils. Thirdly, the boundaries of electoral districts were re-drawn to make sure that the largest possible number of Unionist councillors were elected. The diagrams opposite explain how this practice of 'gerrymandering' was carried out. In Londonderry, for example, there were about 9,000 Protestant voters and 14,000 Catholics voters. After gerrymandering the City Council consisted of 12 Unionists and only 8 Nationalist councillors.

Unionist Councils favoured Protestants when houses were being allocated, and when job vacancies had to be filled. Nationalist Councils felt the same obligation to 'look after our own'. Businessmen acted in the same way, but as there were more Unionist employers it was always easier for Protestants to get jobs, and this caused a great deal of bitterness during the depression of the 1930s. The Unionist Party made no secret of this religious and political discrimination. James Craig, who had been made Lord Craigavon in 1926, quite openly stated in 1934, 'All I boast of is, that we are a Protestant Parliament and a Protestant State'.

The Nationalist MPs who took their places in the Northern Ireland Parliament after 1925, led by Joseph Devlin, had a hopeless task. In most countries a parliamentary opposition can look forward to the time when they will win a general election and form a government. Not so

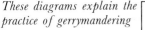

These diagrams explain the practice of gerrymandering

The thirty-six squares represent an area with a population large enough to elect FOUR councillors. Each white square represents a certain number of Nationalist voters and each shaded square represents the same number of Unionist voters. There are eighteen white squares and eighteen shaded squares. You might think that TWO Nationalist councillors and TWO Unionist councillors would be a fair representation for the whole area. But if there are to be four councillors, the area must be divided into four districts, and one councillor elected in each district.

If the area is simply divided four-square there will be THREE Nationalists and ONE Unionist.

It is possible to make a slight alteration which would achieve an equal balance.

It is also possible by drawing the boundaries differently to secure the election of THREE Unionists and ONE Nationalist.

in Northern Ireland. Ten or twelve Nationalist MPs could bring the grievances of the Catholics before Parliament but they could not exercise any effective pressure. The British Parliament at Westminster had authority to overrule the Belfast Parliament, but this was never used. Of the twelve Northern Ireland MPs who sat in the House of Commons, only two were Nationalists; and the House of Commons spent, on average, only two hours per year discussing Northern Ireland.

As there seemed no way of improving conditions for Catholics in the North nor of being reunited with the South by democratic methods, many Catholics were willing to support the IRA or at least not betray it to the authorities. In fact, at times the presence of armed IRA men was welcomed, when they acted to defend Catholic areas in Belfast against mobs of Orange rioters. Catholics generally did not trust the police to protect them, as the RUC and the B Specials were almost all Protestants.

Northern Ireland in the Second World War

In May 1938 Britain agreed to pay Northern Ireland enough money each year to raise government spending on social welfare to British standards. The Belfast Government had been asking for this for many years. It seemed significant that the promise came a few days after Britain had handed back her naval bases in Eire to de Valera. With the threat of war with Germany looming, Northern Ireland had suddenly become strategically important.

When the war broke out it brought very important changes. Industries were put on a war footing. Ships could not be built fast enough. Short and Harland's aircraft factory, opened in 1938, had orders to supply planes; engineering works were producing tanks and other military equipment. Linen mills and the shirt factories of Londonderry were adapted to manufacture uniforms, overalls, and parachutes. Farmers were urged to produce more food, cereals rather than meat, and were given free technical advice.

This rapid transformation of industry and agriculture meant a tremendous increase in jobs; the numbers employed in shipbuilding almost trebled, in the aircraft industry they went from 5800 in 1938 to 23,500 in 1945. The unemployment rate dropped to 5 per cent. Ports had to be developed as naval bases to protect Britain's Atlantic convoys, and when the United States entered the war more airfields

US troops marching to camp after landing in Northern Ireland, January 1942

were laid out. The first American GIs arrived early in 1942, and there was an enormous build-up of Allied forces in Northern Ireland, undergoing training for the D-Day landings in 1944.

Men and women from Northern Ireland joined the British Armed Services in large numbers, though (after much discussion) conscription was not imposed. The civilian population had to put up with the same rationing, shortages, black-out and other discomforts of wartime Britain. They also suffered badly from German air-raids, the heaviest ones being on Belfast in April and May 1941. In the first raid, over 700 people were killed and more than twice as many injured.

The shared dangers and hardships, the economic contribution to the war-effort, and the part played in sea and air defence of North Atlantic shipping all made Northern Ireland appear before the ordinary people of Britain as a loyal and trusty friend. On the other hand, British people only grudgingly accepted the South's neutrality. British politicians and people all felt that Northern Ireland, which had behaved as part of Britain during the war, deserved to be rewarded after the war. In 1945 the new Labour Government in Britain announced that the great improvements in health, welfare and education which were being planned for the British people would also be carried out in Northern Ireland, with the British Treasury paying whatever extra money was required.

13

The Irish Republic to 1973

Economic and social developments

The Second World War, and the changed outlook of the post-war world, had a profound effect on the Republic. In 1943, in a radio broadcast, de Valera looked back on the Ireland of his dreams as

> 'the home of people who valued material wealth only as a basis for right living; of a people who, satisfied with frugal comfort, devoted their leisure to the things of the spirit . . .'

In post-war Ireland, however, not many people shared this ideal. Thousands had personal experience of working in British industries or in the Services during the war, and after the war Irish businessmen and tourists renewed contacts with the rest of Western Europe. The British Labour Government and other governments in Europe were making great efforts, with United States' financial help, to repair war damage and to create better conditions of housing, health, education and leisure for everyone. Irish people wanted to obtain the same conditions for themselves.

The Inter-Party Government of 1948 set the pace with a drive to eradicate tuberculosis. This was carried out by the Minister of Health, Dr Noel Browne, whose own parents and a brother and sister had died of the disease. A housing programme was begun to eliminate slums, and a mother-and-child maternity welfare scheme was proposed in 1950. This was criticised by the Irish Medical Association, and opposed by the Catholic Church, as state interference with the rights of the family. Dr Browne was not supported by the other ministers, and had to resign. The scheme was abandoned, but a modified version was begun by the next Fianna Fail Government in 1951.

During the 1950s and 1960s the Dail passed many health and welfare acts which gave the Republic a form of 'welfare state', providing medical treatment, pensions, and unemployment and sickness benefits. These were at roughly two-thirds of the British level. Education was also improved, the school system reorganised and more money spent by the State to provide free secondary education for all children, free school transport, and a big increase in free university places.

To have more money to spend on health, welfare and education, Irish governments had to increase taxation and this was only possible if people were making more money from agriculture and industry. The Inter-Party Government began a long-term Land Reclamation Scheme and set up new authorities to develop industry and encourage exports, but actual results were slow to follow. Such modernisation of farming as there was merely reduced the number of farm workers needed, and there was not enough factory work in country towns to provide jobs. The population continued to decline as more and more young adults went to find work in Britain, where there was a shortage of labour.

Then, in 1958, the Government decided to try out a five-year plan for the economy, the Economic Development Programme. This was drawn up by a senior Civil Servant, T. K. Whitaker, and was carried out by the new Fianna Fail leader, Sean Lemass, who took over when de Valera retired in 1959. The Whitaker Programme meant spending an extra £53.4 million over five years, and offering grants and tax reliefs to foreign firms. British, American, German, Dutch and Japanese businessmen were soon beginning to open factories of all kinds in the Republic, and people were talking of an 'economic miracle'. Investment in industry almost doubled, emigration fell from 14.8 per 1000 to 5.7 per 1000 and the population actually increased by 62,000 between 1961 and 1966. Exports rose by over 50 per cent.

Allenwood power station, County Kildare. One of eleven peat-fired power stations, it burns 260,000 tonnes of peat a year, producing 190 million units of electricity

The Second Programme for Economic Expansion, published in 1963, planned even faster growth. Its over-optimistic targets were not achieved, but the Irish economy, particularly its industry, continued to expand. In 1973 Ireland, in common with Britain, joined the European Economic Community, which encouraged exports to Europe, and benefited farming through guaranteed prices and other assistance. Ireland rapidly became less dependent on the British market, exports to Britain falling from 75 per cent of total exports in 1960 to 47 per cent in 1977.

Religion and nationalism

Up to the outbreak of the Second World War in 1939 the two main distinguishing marks of the Irish Free State were its Gaelic nationalism and its Catholic religion. After the war both of these changed.

Before the war Catholics in Ireland had always accepted the views of the bishops on moral and social questions, though not always on political matters. In the 1950s Irish Catholic bishops remained very conservative and expected unquestioning obedience, but they found people more ready to think for themselves, and less hesitant about saying what they thought.

The Catholic Church as a whole was changing, as shown by the more liberal outlook of Pope John XXIII and the free-ranging discussions of the Second Vatican Council of 1962. The Ecumenical Movement also affected the churches in Ireland, with clergy laying more stress on features of Christianity common to all churches, and taking part in joint services.

These changes were welcomed in the Irish Republic, especially by young adults who had the advantage of better education and more contact with other countries. A more informed and open-minded attitude was encouraged by Telefis Eireann, the Irish Television service, which was launched on New Year's Eve 1962. This, along with British Television available in Dublin and the eastern counties, led people to accept the airing of views on sex, birth control, censorship and other topics. There was, however, a limit to permissiveness. Censorship continued, although it was less active. Divorce was still not recognised by law and legal obstacles were put in the way of family planning. At the same time, active pressure-groups demanded that these laws should be changed, and that the Church should change its teaching also. There was no significant decline in Church membership, but a growing number believed that Catholic morality should be accepted by devout Catholics of their own choice, and not imposed by law. In 1972 a referendum decided that the 'special position' given to the Church by the 1937 Constitution (see page 70) should be ended. However, a proposal to legalise divorce was rejected by a referendum in 1986.

Gaelic nationalism also changed after the war. Gaelic was retained as an official language, but state pressure for its use in schools was eased. Governments still expressed hopes for the revival of Gaelic, but had to accept that most people did not see its revival as being of vital importance. Other aspects of Gaelic culture flourished: Irish music, Irish dancing and particularly sports under the guidance of the GAA (see page 30). The GAA, however, dropped its ban on 'foreign games'.

The traditional nationalist view of Irish history was also modified. The history of Ireland had previously been seen more or less as a succession of political and military battles against British oppression. In each period of struggle there were heroic figures to be admired. In the 1960s and 1970s a more realistic attitude spread from the universities to schools and the general public. History books had more to say about economic and social developments, different points of view were explained, and the old heroes like O'Connell and Parnell were looked at in a more critical light.

The post-war generation showed little interest in the bitter quarrels of the 1920s: a cartoon from Dublin Opinion, *June 1959*

" Civil war ! What civil war, Deirdre ? "

World affairs

When the Republic became a member of the United Nations in 1956, Irish delegates took a strictly neutral line, sometimes to the annoyance of the USA. In general they followed the attitude of de Valera in the pre-war League of Nations: that small nations should stand together and insist that the super-powers keep to the spirit of the organisation. For this the Republic won the admiration of many emerging African and Asian states, especially because on many occasions Irish troops made up part of a UN Peace-Keeping Force. The largest contingen was sent in 1960 to the Congo, where twenty-six men were killed and many wounded in the task of enforcing the authority of the United Nations.

In 1962 the new Government of Sean Lemass made it clear that the Republic would side with the United States in any confrontation with the USSR, and President J. F. Kennedy had an enthusiastic welcome when he visited Ireland in 1963. Entry into the Common Market and representation in the European Parliament led to Ireland's greater participation in European politics.

The Republic and Partition

The years after the Second World War saw a general movement of de-colonisation in Asia and Africa, with states such as Britain and France, often reluctantly, allowing former colonies to become independent. Opinion in the United States strongly supported this process. In the Irish Republic, Northern Ireland was widely regarded as a British colony, with an oppressive government depending on British support, and a general attack on Partition began.

The Anti-Partition League carried on a propaganda campaign which was backed by Fianna Fail, Fine Gael and the other parties. De Valera, when he was leader of the Opposition in 1948, toured the United States, Australia and Britain, speaking against Partition. The Inter-Party Government instructed its diplomats to raise the question as often as possible at international conferences. None of this had much effect on the British view that Partition was a matter for the two Irish Governments. The Unionists in Northern Ireland still wished to remain separate – even more when the South, once 'associated with' the Commonwealth, became the Republic of Ireland and legally a foreign state in 1949. One important result however, was that the Republic refused to join NATO in 1949, because Britain was regarded as respon-sible for keeping Ireland divided.

The Anti-Partition campaign petered out after some time, leaving its supporters in the Republic and in the Six Counties very disap-pointed. This helped to bring about a revival of the IRA. Young men who saw that peaceful protests achieved nothing felt that in the IRA they would be able to do something. In 1952 raids to secure arms and explosives began, and from 1956 to 1961 a number of attacks were made on police and on customs posts and other buildings along the border. The Garda in the Republic and the RUC in the North were taken by surprise, but they soon began to co-operate so effectively that IRA men had to concentrate on merely avoiding capture. There was some sympathy in the Republic for the IRA men who were killed, but no real approval of their actions. The IRA also found at this time that they could no longer depend on the automatic loyalty of Catholics in Northern Ireland. In 1962 the IRA campaign was called off.

In 1965 Sean Lemass, the Fianna Fail Prime Minister, made what most people in the Republic thought was a more acceptable and realistic move towards ending Partition. An exchange of visits was arranged between him and the Northern Ireland Prime Minister, Terence O'Neill, the first such direct contact since 1922. They agreed to co-operate on such matters as tourism and electricity supply. Both states were hoping to join the Common Market in the near future, and if they could work together for economic prosperity people on both sides of the Border would benefit. These promising signs came to nothing in 1969, when the majority in Northern Ireland rejected O'Neill's leadership, and he resigned.

When violence broke out in Northern Ireland (see Chapter 14) there was, for a time, a wave of old-fashioned nationalism in the Republic. Some TDs were ready to support armed intervention in the North, to protect the Catholics there. The Irish Prime Minister, Jack Lynch, managed to win support for a more cautious policy, however. He showed the deep concern which people in the Republic felt, by vigorous complaints to the Governments of Britain and Northern Ireland about the treatment of prisoners, suspects, and the Catholic population in general, by the security forces.

14

Northern Ireland to 1972

British welfare

As promised, after the Second World War the British 'welfare state' was extended to Northern Ireland, with the British Treasury providing all the extra money needed to establish health, welfare and education at the same standard as in Britain. From 1961 to 1963 the average payment was £60 million per year. This rose to about £126 million in 1967–8 and went up to at least £160 million by 1971–2. It was estimated that the Republic would have to more than double taxation in order to provide an equal level of social services for its citizens. In addition, the British government helped to encourage new industries. This was necessary because while agriculture continued to prosper, Northern Ireland's industries rapidly declined. Even with new factories opening unemployment was high; nearly 7 per cent in 1969, when the average for the United Kingdom was just over 2 per cent.

New firms were concentrated in the Belfast area, but the western and southern districts contained a bigger proportion of Catholics. Protestant employers still preferred Protestant workers. These were two reasons why unemployment was felt more keenly by Catholic families. In addition, Catholics resented the ways in which many Unionist Councils discriminated against them in housing and other local services.

In Britain since the war every adult had a vote in council elections, but in Northern Ireland voting was still restricted to householders and property-owners. Young unmarried adults therefore felt cheated at being unable to influence local councils, and wanted the 'democratic rights' which were being talked about so much in the post-war world.

The demand for British democracy

The Homeless Citizens League was formed in Dungannon, County Tyrone, in 1963. Its object was to shame the local council into providing more houses for Catholic families. When it succeeded, it developed into the Campaign for Social Justice, investigating cases of religious discrimination all over Northern Ireland. In 1967 the campaign formed the nucleus of the Civil Rights Association, which set out to do more than just try to deal with particular cases.

The Civil Rights Association, or CRA, copied the methods used in the 1960s: in America to obtain equal rights for blacks, and in Europe by student protesters. They held marches by thousands of people, and mass open-air meetings. They tried to get as much publicity as possible, especially through television, which brought events before the public much faster than the old cinema newsreels and with more impact than radio. The CRA's main demand was for the same voting rights as people had in local council elections in Britain. In the words of the popular chant: 'One man, one vote'.

The Prime Minister of Northern Ireland at this time was Terence O'Neill, who succeeded Sir Basil Brooke in 1963. Brooke, later Lord Brookeborough, had been Prime Minister and leader of the Unionist Party since 1943. Brooke had continued in the tradition of Sir James Craig, but O'Neill believed that changes were overdue. O'Neill was keen to encourage better relations between Catholics and Protestants, and to remove some of the social hardships of working-class Catholics.

Terence O'Neill (nearest camera) visiting a Catholic school in April 1964. He was the first Northern Ireland Prime Minister ever to do so. This press photograph showing the crucifix threw extreme Protestants into a fury

He also wanted to treat the Republic as a friendly neighbour, while keeping Northern Ireland within the United Kingdom. Many Unionists, however, could see no need to give Catholics fairer treatment, and the old fears of Home Rule times began to revive. The Orange Order became more active, and in 1966 the Ulster Volunteer Force was secretly re-established.

The first Civil Rights march in Dungannon in the summer of 1968 passed off peacefully, but a CRA march in Londonderry in October was broken up by the RUC on the orders of William Craig, the Home Secretary, who was later dismissed from the Cabinet by O'Neill. This was followed by the formation of the Derry Citizens' Action Committee, whose chief spokesman was John Hume; and the People's Democracy, a socialist group of students, whose aims were voiced by Bernadette Devlin. Counter-marches and demonstrations were carried on by extreme Unionists, generally organised by the Reverend Ian Paisley, the leader of a breakaway sect, the Free Presbyterian Church. He had founded this himself in 1951, believing that ecumenical ideas were weakening Protestant resistance to Catholicism.

In January 1969 a march from Belfast to Londonderry organised by the People's Democracy was attacked by Protestants at Burntollet Bridge. The RUC and B Specials took little effective action to protect the marchers, and some of the police themselves joined in a general attack on the Catholic Bogside district of Londonderry when the march finally got through. In April O'Neill persuaded a majority of Unionist MPs to agree to the CRA demand of 'One man, one vote', but he continued to lose the support of his Party and Protestants generally, and he resigned in May 1969.

His successors were James Chichester-Clark up to March 1971 and Brian Faulkner from March 1971 to March 1972. Both Prime Ministers continued O'Neill's policy of equal rights for Catholics. Commissioners were appointed to investigate complaints against central and local government officials. Fair rules were enforced about the allocation of council houses. The B Specials were disbanded and the RUC were disarmed. Local government was completely re-organised and further efforts were made to develop the economy and reduce unemployment. In 1971 Brian Faulkner began a new system of Parliamentary Committees to give non-Unionist MPs some real influence on government policy. In this way the first member of the Northern Ireland Labour Party and the first Catholic were able to take their places as members of the Government of Northern Ireland. The British Government supported these reforms, even insisting on some of them. Unfortunately, however, the reforms took place against a rapid worsening of violence on the streets of Northern Ireland's cities and towns.

Outrage and retaliation

The Protestant middle and upper class had run the Six Counties since Partition in 1921. The Protestant working class had suffered a great deal of hardship and neglect, but through the years of bad housing, ill-health and unemployment they kept the conviction that they had the 'right' religion at least. They believed that they counted for more than the Catholics and that they had the right to a better share of any benefits, such as houses or jobs. O'Neill's policy from 1963 onwards meant that Catholics would no longer be 'second class' citizens, and this made ordinary Protestants feel that they were going to lose their favoured position. They responded, therefore, by trying in the traditional way to frighten the Catholics into submission.

A Civil Rights demonstration might be regarded in British streets merely as an attempt to obtain publicity for a certain point of view. In Belfast or Londonderry, Protestants saw it as organised Catholics directly challenging the dominance of the Protestants. It was an instinct of Northern Ireland Protestants to 'show them who was boss'. As the Unionist government, led by O'Neill, was apparently too ready to agree to Catholic demands, Protestant people were quite prepared to take the necessary action themselves. Independent investigation found that even trained and disciplined members of the RUC were at times overcome by this feeling.

After the affair at Burntollet Bridge in January 1969 there was comparative quiet, but during the summer there were serious riots in Belfast following the Orange parades on 12 July, and in Londonderry in August. Protestant rioters attacked Catholic districts and burned down 500 houses. Hundreds were injured on both sides and ten people died. The RUC, outnumbered and quite unable to restore order, was again accused of directing most force against the Catholics. Fearing a complete breakdown of law and order, the British Prime Minister, Harold Wilson, ordered British troops to Belfast and Londonderry on 15 August 1969. Their job was to protect the Catholic minority from attack and support peace-keeping by the police. Following the disbanding of the B Specials a new local Army Regiment was established, the UDR or Ulster Defence Regiment. At first, British troops were welcomed in the Catholic areas, especially when they were used against Protestant extremists who opposed the reforms in the RUC in October. Within less than a year of their arrival, however, they had lost the trust of the Catholics, partly because of the appearance of a new force, the Provisional IRA.

The Provisionals

The IRA's campaign along the Border in the late 1950s had been called off mainly because of lack of support from Northern Ireland Catholics. The benefits of the welfare state made the idea of joining in an All-Ireland Republic less attractive to many; the Civil Rights movement aimed at winning equality within Northern Ireland, not at overthrowing the state.

After 1962 the IRA itself was divided over what its policy should be. Many of the leaders felt that they should regain popular support

HERE AT PEACE
THE 'SPECIALS'
RECLINE —
CONDEMNED BY
HUNT IN '69

← ARMY HQ
R.U.C HQ →

After the Hunt Report in 1969 the B Specials were disbanded, but there were doubts in the Republic about the new non-sectarian UDR. A cartoon from Dublin Opinion, *December 1969*

in the Republic as well as in the North, by becoming active in matters of social concern such as housing and unemployment. A few individuals took an interest in the Civil Rights movement, but during the attacks on Catholic areas in Belfast and Londonderry in 1969 the IRA offered no leadership nor protection. Stinging criticism was painted up on walls in Catholic streets: IRA = I Ran Away. The Northern section of the IRA blamed the Army Council in Dublin. In December 1969, at the IRA Convention in Dublin, a group calling themselves the Provisional IRA broke away and set up their own separate Army

Council. Sinn Fein, the political wing of the IRA, also split into 'Provisionals' and 'Officials'.

The Provisionals followed the traditional ideas of the IRA. They began recruiting throughout Northern Ireland, and arming themselves to defend the Catholic population from Protestant attack. To them Britain was the enemy, and the presence of British troops in Ireland could not be tolerated. After their rough treatment at the hands of Protestant rioters the Catholics were now more willing to shelter IRA men, and conceal weapons. This, in turn, led to troops searching Catholic houses for guns and, when they met resistance, using CS riot gas to disperse the hostile crowds. The searches, and the use of CS gas in Catholic areas, made people there see the troops as oppressors, no different from the old B Specials. This made it easier for the Provisional IRA to gain yet more recruits, and present themselves as the only protection for the Catholic people. Protestants, seeing the alliance between the IRA and the people in Catholic working-class areas such as the Falls Road in Belfast, took it as proof that the IRA had been behind the Civil Rights movement from the very beginning of the unrest in 1963.

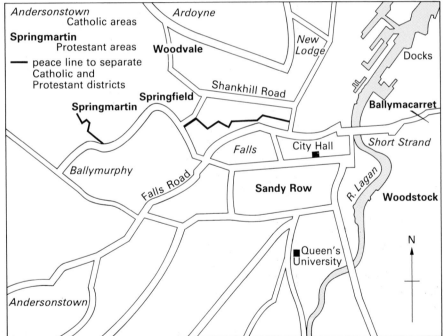

Belfast, showing the main Protestant and Catholic districts of the city

The first British soldier to be killed in Northern Ireland was shot by the IRA in February 1971. After April the Provisionals tended to avoid deliberate ambushes of Army patrols and concentrated on a bombing campaign, directed against police and army posts, public buildings, factories, shops, hotels and public houses. The object of this was to kill or injure soldiers or policemen, damage government property and harass the authorities generally.

The end of Stormont

In August 1970 a group of moderate Catholic MPs in the Northern Ireland Parliament at Stormont came together to form a new party, the Social Democratic and Labour Party, or SDLP. Its leading members were Gerry Fitt, an experienced member of the Northern Ireland Labour Party, and John Hume of the CRA. Their immediate aim was to get fair treatment for Catholics and better economic and social conditions for the working class in general, but they hoped for the eventual re-unification of Ireland by peaceful means. The SDLP was invited by Brian Faulkner, in June 1971, to accept the chairmanship of two new committees dealing with social and economic problems. This would give them direct influence on government policy. Before they accepted, however, two Catholic civilians were killed by soldiers in Londonderry. The SDLP, representing moderate Catholic opinion, demanded that the British Government should hold an immediate enquiry into the killing. When this was not done, the SDLP walked out of the Stormont Parliament.

Unable through this to get the co-operation of moderate Catholics, Faulkner turned to the customary way of separating the IRA from the Catholic population, by rounding up all known and suspected IRA members, and interning them without trial under the Special Powers Act. This was done in August 1971, but the RUC failed to net all the IRA and arrested many innocent people. In protest, about 20,000 Catholics on council estates joined in a rent-and-rates strike. This lasted for three years.

In the first months of 1972 Northern Ireland seemed to be on the brink of civil war. Middle-class and generally moderate Catholics were protesting against internment and the Army's rough handling of working-class Catholics. Working-class Catholics were demonstrating in the streets, where they were often in battle with police and soldiers. The Protestant working class were joining extremist action groups, which looked more and more menacing. The largest of these was the Ulster Defence Association, or UDA, founded in August 1971. Shooting incidents and murders continued. The IRA bombing campaign went on, now extended to cities in England. British troops found themselves in a position where there was no clear enemy, but where anyone on either the Catholic or Protestant side might become one.

In an atmosphere of extreme tension, British troops shot dead thirteen unarmed civilians during a Civil Rights march in Londonderry on Sunday 30 January 1972. Bloody Sunday, shown on television, strengthened the impression that the situation was fast running out of control. Moderate people throughout the British Isles were shocked. In the Republic there was a call for armed intervention by the Irish Army. In Northern Ireland the Prime Minister, Brian Faulkner, was losing the support of Unionist MPs as their Party split into smaller and more extreme groups.

For some time Britain had been warning the Unionists that by the

A UDA parade through Belfast, May 1972

Government of Ireland Act of 1920, the United Kingdom Parliament still had supreme authority. The old, apparently unshakeable rule of Protestant Unionists had broken down rapidly since 1969. The dominance of the Unionist Party could not be restored, and, in spite of O'Neill's reforms, the Catholics were in no mood to return quickly to quiet, law-abiding respectability. On 24 March 1972, Edward Heath, the British Prime Minister, suspended the Stormont Parliament and direct rule from Britain was imposed.

PART FIVE

THE PRESENT TROUBLES

15

Northern Ireland, Britain and the Irish Republic 1972–86

The collapse of power-sharing 1972–4

Most people hoped that direct rule would do two things. It might make Unionists, or Loyalists as they were now being called, co-operate with British plans to set up a system of government on a new basis in Northern Ireland. It might also reassure Catholics that they would be fully protected, and have the same rights as any citizen of the United Kingdom.

British Governments on many occasions had promised that Northern Ireland would remain part of the United Kingdom so long as a majority of people there agreed. The Six Counties included a population which was now 61 per cent Protestant/Unionist and 39 per cent Catholic/Nationalist, and these proportions were not likely to change in the foreseeable future. The British Government recognised that there would not be harmony between the two communities unless the majority accepted the views of the minority to some extent, and the minority felt that their opinions were being listened to and given some recognition.

The plan adopted by William Whitelaw, Secretary of State for Northern Ireland, was for a form of power-sharing between Protestants and Catholics in an Assembly of elected representatives. This was accepted by the main Unionist Party (Official Unionists) and the SDLP, but the extreme Loyalist Groups and the extreme Catholics (Provisional Sinn Fein) rejected it. The Government of the Irish Republic, whose views were now being considered, also supported the idea of power-sharing. The Assembly elections were held in 1973 and the power-sharing government, the Executive, took over in January 1974, made up of seven Official Unionists, six SDLP members, and three members of the Alliance Party which was not identified with any religious group. About the same time, in December 1973, a conference was held at Sunningdale in England between representatives of Britain, the Republic and the Northern Ireland Executive. They agreed that a Council of Ireland should be set up to encourage co-operation in economic progress, human rights and law enforcement in both parts of Ireland.

In the general election in February 1974, however, out of the twelve Northern Ireland seats in the British House of Commons, eleven were won by extreme Unionists. Northern Ireland's Protestant majority were angry at the idea of power-sharing, and at the British view that opinion in the Irish Republic should be taken into account. A new organisation, the Ulster Workers' Council, representing the Protestant working class was formed, and it called a general strike. This paralysed Northern Ireland, and demonstrated that the power-sharing Executive was, in fact, powerless without the support of the majority of the people. In May 1974 the Executive resigned, the Sunningdale Agreement lapsed, and direct rule from Britain was restored. Britain made no further moves in this direction until 1985.

The IRA and Sinn Fein

The IRA always regarded itself as being in a state of war against Britain. From 1969 onwards the Provisional IRA kept up a campaign of bombing and shooting directed against the RUC, troops, prison officers, magistrates and judges in Northern Ireland. Bombs were also exploded in public buildings and streets as a challenge to the authorities and to gain publicity. The IRA expressed regret for civilian deaths and injuries but regarded them as unavoidable in a war.

In the 1970s the bombing campaign was extended to Britain, with the main targets in London and Birmingham. Bombs in two Birmingham public houses in 1974 killed 19 people and injured 182. In 1979 Airey Neave MP, the Conservative Party spokesman on Northern Ireland, was killed by a bomb in his car at the House of Commons. The same year Lord Mountbatten, Queen Elizabeth's uncle, was killed at his holiday home in County Sligo in the Irish Republic. In 1982 two bombs were exploded in London, killing soldiers of the Horse Guards and military bandsmen in Hyde Park and Regent's Park. In September 1984 a bomb in the Grand Hotel, Brighton, demolished part of the building and killed one MP and four other leading members of the Conservative Party. The main targets, who escaped death, were the Prime Minister, Margaret Thatcher, and members of the Government who had assembled for the Conservative Party Conference.

Sinn Fein, the political party which represents the views of the IRA, refused to take part in central or local government elections until 1981 because they did not accept British rule in Ireland as legitimate. This made it difficult to assess how much real popular support they had. In November 1981 the Sinn Fein conference decided to campaign 'with a ballot paper in one hand and an Armalite rifle in the other'. In subsequent local council elections Sinn Fein candidates took votes from the SDLP. In 1983 the Sinn Fein candidate, Gerry Adams, defeated the SDLP leader, Gerry Fitt, to become MP for West Belfast. By

The damaged front of the Grand Hotel, Brighton, October 1984

November 1985 Sinn Fein also had fifty-nine local councillors and their share of the total number of votes in council elections was 12 per cent, compared with the SDLP's 18 per cent.

Unionists were outraged at having to accept members of Sinn Fein as fellow councillors, and tried various ways of excluding them from Council meetings. Having failed, seventeen Councils with Unionist majorities decided not to meet at all. Another result of Sinn Fein electoral success was that the SDLP felt compelled to try to win back Nationalist voters by showing more urgency to end Partition, while continuing to work for social and religious equality.

People of Irish origin in the United States contributed money to help distressed Catholic families in Northern Ireland when the troubles began in 1969. Most of this was channelled through an organisation called Noraid, and its distribution in Northern Ireland was carried out in collaboration with Sinn Fein. This practical help was important in winning support for Sinn Fein, but it was widely suspected that some of Noraid's funds were being used to buy arms and explosives for the IRA.

Although Sinn Fein had success in elections, the IRA continued its attacks on troops and police and took no notice of moves by London and Dublin to try to reach a solution of the Northern Ireland problem. Sinn Fein and the IRA hoped to compel Britain to give up responsibility for Northern Ireland, leading to the establishment of a full thirty-two county republic. Anything less than that would not be acceptable.

Britain's response to terrorism

The British priority in the 1970s was to prevent IRA attacks and to find and punish anyone who took part in them. Ordinary methods of policing and trial were not effective enough, so special measures were taken, although these were often criticised as denying the rights of citizens of a democratic country in peacetime.

The widespread use of regiments of the British Army in patrols, security checks, arms-searches and riot-control was regarded as necessary in the early 1970s. In July 1972 there were 21,000 British troops in Northern Ireland, but these were gradually reduced. By 1985 their numbers were down to about 9000. Meanwhile the RUC was made more effective with improved training, better equipment and larger numbers. The Ulster Defence Regiment, recruited and serving only in Northern Ireland, was built up from its foundation in 1970. It was used for guard duties on essential installations such as power stations, and to assist the RUC. It was hoped that both the RUC and the UDR would reflect the 60 per cent–40 per cent proportion of Protestants and Catholics in the population. Threats and shootings of Catholic recruits by the IRA, however, increased the natural reluctance of Catholics to join Protestant security forces. The percentage of Catholics in the RUC remained at 10 per cent; and in the UDR at 3 per cent.

When suspected terrorists were arrested by police or soldiers it was very difficult to find people willing to give evidence against them. Neither Republicans nor Loyalists would co-operate with the courts because of a sense of group loyalty. Others who might have been willing to act as prosecution witnesses were often afraid to do so for fear of reprisal. It was found also that a Catholic jury would not condemn a Catholic prisoner, nor a jury of Protestants a Protestant. On the recommendation of Lord Diplock who investigated the situation in 1972, special courts were set up to deal with terrorist offences. These Diplock courts have a single judge and no jury. Courts in Northern Ireland also obtained convictions on the sole evidence of a 'supergrass' – a convicted terrorist who was persuaded to give evidence against large numbers of his former associates. 'Diplock' courts and 'supergrass' trials are regarded by both Catholics and Protestants as lacking the normal requirements of justice. The 'supergrass' system also broke down when appeal courts ruled that their evidence was not reliable enough.

Another weapon against terrorism was introduced in 1974 after the 'Birmingham pub' bombings. This was the Prevention of Terrorism Act which gave the police in Britain wider powers of arrest and detention in cases of terrorist suspects. It also allowed the Home Secretary to ban the entry into Britain of any person from Northern Ireland or the Irish Republic and to deport anyone suspected of being engaged in terrorist activities. The expulsion of a British citizen from one part of the United Kingdom to another was widely seen as illogical.

Even before 1969, Unionists in Northern Ireland complained that members of the IRA who had committed crimes in the Six Counties could escape across the border and be free in the Twenty-Six Counties. This was because the courts there would not extradite anyone wanted by the Northern Ireland authorities if the offence was considered to be political. (Similar safeguards would have applied to a citizen of Northern Ireland committing a political crime in the Twenty-Six Counties, if any such cases had occurred.) In the Sunningdale Agreement of 1973 (see page 92) the Irish Government agreed to co-operate in a study of extradition but when the Agreement was abandoned nothing more was done until 1982. In that year the Irish Supreme Court redefined the legal interpretation of 'political offences', and the British authorities took the opportunity to test the willingness of the Republic to hand over people charged with offences in Northern Ireland or Britain. In the first such case, Dominic McGlinchey was extradited to Northern Ireland in 1984 but was found not guilty of the charges and had to be handed back to the Republic in 1985 to face trial there for other offences. Another wanted man could not be extradited because the necessary documents had not been made out correctly by the Northern Ireland authorities. A third was extradited but acquitted by the court in Belfast. In March 1986 Evelyn Glenholmes, wanted in connection with bomb outrages in London, was arrested but had to be set free again in Dublin because the extradition warrants made out in London were inaccurate. Up to 1986 therefore, extradition had not resulted in large numbers of terrorists having to stand trial and face well-deserved punishment, as was expected by Northern Ireland Loyalists.

The Irish Republic

The Irish Republic in the 1970s and early 1980s continued to develop economically and socially along the lines laid down in the 1960s. As an industrial country exporting worldwide it was affected by the problems common to all such countries – high oil prices and the recession in world trade. The Industrial Development Authority continued its success in encouraging foreign investment in the electronics, pharmaceutical, and food processing industries. Jobs in these and other 'high-tech' industries increased from 3000 in 1974 to 21,000 in 1984. At the same time, more traditional industries, such as clothing and furniture, suffered competition from imports, and the population continued to increase. Governments were faced with the problems of inflation and unemployment and had to decide whether to reduce state spending and reduce taxation, or to increase taxes and improve social benefits. In 1981 it was estimated that about 20 per cent of the population was on, or below, the poverty line. In most people's minds the question of re-unification of Ireland came far behind the need to decide the best policies on unemployment, wages, and taxes.

Yet Northern Ireland and the treatment of Catholics/Nationalists there remained a persistent, if not a pressing, problem. There was still an underlying belief that Ireland should be one state. Bombings and shootings in the North tended to discourage foreign investment and tourism in the Republic as well. The IRA carried out a number of robberies and kidnappings in the Republic to get money. These, and searches for arms by the Garda and the Irish army, sometimes resulted in shoot-outs and some deaths. Trouble and expense were involved in patrolling the border, following up information about arms dumps and capturing ships like the *Claudia* in 1973 with five tonnes of arms and explosives from Libya, and the trawler *Marita Anne* in 1984, loaded with weapons from America. Irish Governments also had to defend their use of special jury-less courts to deal with IRA suspects, and their ban on radio and television interviews by any extremist leaders.

The New Ireland Forum

By 1984 Britain seemed to be no nearer a political solution in Northern Ireland, and no more likely to defeat the IRA by police and military action. Sinn Fein were gaining Catholic votes in the North at the expense of the SDLP and might therefore be encouraged to take part in electoral politics in the Republic. The Irish Prime Minister, Garrett FitzGerald, proposed a series of meetings, the New Ireland Forum, to work out an agreement on the future of Ireland. All the parties in the

Republic were represented, and the SDLP from Northern Ireland. Sinn Fein was not invited. The Unionist parties were invited but refused to take part. In May 1984 the Forum produced three possible plans. The recommended one was that there should be a single thirty-two-county Republic of Ireland, with constitutional guarantees of respect for the Protestant religion, traditions and outlook. Another suggestion was for a federal arrangement with two separate regional parliaments for the areas of the Twenty-Six Counties and the Six Counties. The third scheme was for a system of joint rule over Northern Ireland by Britain and the Republic, which might satisfy the desire of the majority in the Six Counties to remain British.

In November, Margaret Thatcher, the British Prime Minister, dismissed all three ideas as impossible, but Britain and Ireland were in fact already trying to reach some other arrangement which would also be acceptable to both religious communities in Northern Ireland.

The Anglo-Irish Agreement

Discussions continued for a further twelve months, with frequent rumours about the likely outcome and increasing fears among Northern Ireland Protestants that their views were being ignored. The talks, and the agreement when it came, were between the Governments of Britain and Ireland only; no political parties were invited to take part. The Agreement (sometimes referred to as the Accord) was signed at Hillsborough Castle in County Down on 15 November 1985.

The Agreement committed both governments to achieve in Northern Ireland a state 'in which all may live in peace, free from discrimination and intolerance', and in which all citizens were to have the opportunity to participate in government. Each community, Protestant and Catholic, was to have the right 'to pursue its aspirations by peaceful and constitutional means'.

The Agreement said that an inter-governmental Conference was to meet regularly to deal with four kinds of things:

1. Political matters.
2. Security, including the need to increase Catholic trust in, and membership of, the RUC.
3. Legal matters, including better extradition arrangements, and the possibility of courts with judges from Northern Ireland and the Republic sitting together.
4. Cross-border co-operation between security forces.

The regular Conference was also to protect the rights and identities of both traditions, Nationalist and Loyalist, and to try to bring about reconciliation, respect for human rights, the suppression of terrorism, and economic, social and cultural co-operation between Northern Ireland and the Republic.

The Agreement was to be reviewed after three years, or earlier if either Government requested it. Also, an inter-parliamentary body of

British MPs and Irish TDs would be set up to discuss matters of mutual concern.

The Anglo-Irish Agreement was welcomed by a majority of all political parties at Westminster, with the exception of the Ulster Unionists. It was accepted by the Dail, although Charles Haughey, the leader of the Fianna Fail opposition, was rather critical. Many people in America, and especially those of Irish descent, were very pleased at the prospect of peace in Northern Ireland. Since 1949 United States governments had been keen for Ireland to join NATO and the Agreement might eventually lead to this. President Reagan proposed to contribute $290 million over five years to help make the Agreement work.

In Northern Ireland the SDLP gave its approval, although most moderate Catholics preferred to wait and see what difference it would make in practice. Sinn Fein and the IRA announced that it would make no difference to their activities. The strongest reaction came from the Protestant community and their MPs in the Unionist parties at Westminster.

The Loyalist backlash

After the first outbreak of violent reaction to the Civil Rights Campaign in 1969 and the General Strike against power-sharing in 1974, Protestant organisations remained more or less passive. Unionist politicians regularly demanded more effective action against the IRA and urged Britain to do more to encourage industry in Northern Ireland. When there was any particularly horrifying IRA or INLA murder, the Unionists warned Britain of the danger of retaliation by extreme Loyalist groups, and occasionally Catholics were killed by such groups in what seemed to be tit-for-tat action. In general, however, the Protestant community was willing to leave the RUC and the UDR to deal with the IRA, and seemed reasonably content with direct rule from Westminster.

The Anglo-Irish talks in 1984 and 1985, however, gave rise to fears that the position of Northern Ireland as part of the United Kingdom would be affected, in spite of British assurances that Britain would retain complete sovereignty. When the Hillsborough Agreement was signed in November 1985 there was an outburst of fury which showed how much fear and distrust existed in the Protestant community.

The Agreement was denounced by the UDA as a 'sell-out' of Loyalists by the British government, allowing the Republic to interfere in Northern Ireland. Loyalists were reported to be 'sickened and stunned'. Death threats against Sinn Fein members were issued by the Protestant Action Force, a previously unknown group. Posters went up, urging people to boycott goods made in the Republic. A huge Unionist rally was held in Belfast, intended to copy the anti-Home Rule demonstrations of 1912 and a protest march took place from Derry to Belfast – the reverse route of the Catholic Civil Rights march of 1969. There were suggestions that Northern Ireland should separate from Britain and become an independent state. An extra 550 British troops were sent to Northern Ireland as a precaution.

The two Unionist leaders, James Molyneux (Official Unionists) and the Rev. Ian Paisley (Democratic Unionists) attempted to have the Agreement declared unconstitutional in the courts, and when that failed, demanded that a referendum should be held so that voters could reject the Agreement. When this was refused, all fifteen Unionist MPs resigned from the House of Commons. They intended that the by-elections which would follow would show that the majority of voters in Northern Ireland were against the Agreement. When the elections were held in January 1986 fourteen Unionist MPs were re-elected, but Seamus Mallon, the Deputy Leader of the SDLP, was elected in one constituency previously held by a Unionist. Overall, the SDLP who were in favour of the Agreement, gained votes at the expense of Sinn Fein. This seemed to show that more Catholics were willing to test the Agreement instead of following the hard line of Sinn Fein who still wanted nothing less than a complete British withdrawal from Northern Ireland.

After the elections, the British Government made an offer of talks with the Unionist leaders, but they refused unless Britain suspended the Agreement. They also called for a one-day strike of workers throughout Northern Ireland, hoping to remind the Government of the strike which had destroyed the power-sharing scheme in 1974. Molyneux and Paisley planned a peaceful strike and Loyalist meetings, but found it impossible to control some of their supporters when the day came, 1 March.

The more extreme Loyalists were not content just to strike themselves, and to persuade other workers to stay out of work. In many places they blocked roads, held up traffic, set fire to cars and fought with the RUC who were trying to remove road-blocks. A further 550 troops were sent to Northern Ireland, bringing the total to over 10,000.

Later in March the RUC were again the target for Loyalist violence, particularly in Portadown, where there had already been trouble in July 1985 over police restrictions on the traditional Orange marches. Since Hillsborough, the RUC were accused of 'taking orders from Dublin' and they were treated as traitors to their fellow Protestants for attempting to prevent intimidation of Catholics. Not only were the RUC attacked in street riots, but those who lived in Protestant districts of Portadown and Belfast found themselves and their families harassed and threatened. In some cases their homes were petrol-bombed and burnt down. The death of a Protestant, Keith White, killed by a plastic bullet during a riot in Portadown, caused even more anger against the RUC and a demand that plastic bullets should be banned. (Fifteen people, seven of them children, had already been killed by rubber or plastic bullets since 1969 – but they were Catholics.)

The leader of the Official Unionist Party, James Molyneux, was shocked by the character of the anti-Agreement strike and by the outbursts of Loyalist violence mostly directed against the RUC. Both he and the Rev. Ian Paisley were worried that they were losing control, and that Northern Ireland would collapse into a condition of religious civil war. To direct Loyalist opposition to the Agreement into more manageable channels, they announced a rate strike at the end of April 1986 and a massive publicity campaign. They also agreed to discuss the possibility of having talks with the British Government, provided the changes intended by the Agreement were not introduced too quickly, nor too insensitively.

Postcript

In the 1840s Thomas Davis stressed the Irishness of Protestants as well as Catholics. He was aware that Ireland was 'inhabited by men of many different races and creeds', but pointed out that there was 'no country on earth where there are not many races mixed into one nation'. He asked, 'Why should the races in Ireland hate and ruin each other because their fathers came here at different times, from different countries?'

In the 1960s Terence O'Neill, speaking of Northern Ireland, made a similar plea:

'Here we are, in this small country of ours, Protestant and Catholic, committed by history to live side by side. No solution based on the ascendancy of any section of our community can hope to endure. Either we live in peace, or we have no life worth living.'

Appendix I
Political parties in Ireland since 1922

	Taoiseach and party in office	Main opposition in Dail	Opposition outside
1922	Griffith/Collins: pro-Treaty Sinn Fein	Labour Party	De Valera: anti-Treaty Sinn Fein
1923	Cosgrave: Cumann na nGaedheal	Labour Party	anti-Treaty Sinn Fein
1927	Cosgrave: Cumann na nGaedheal	De Valera: Fianna Fail	IRA/Sinn Fein
1932	De Valera: Fianna Fail	Cosgrave: Fine Gael (founded Sept. 1933)	IRA/Sinn Fein
1948	Costello: (Fine Gael) Inter-Party Government	Fianna Fail	IRA/Sinn Fein
1951	De Valera: Fianna Fail	Fine Gael	IRA/Sinn Fein
1954	Costello: Inter-Party Government	Fianna Fail	IRA/Sinn Fein
1957	De Valera: Fianna Fail	Fine Gael	IRA/Sinn Fein
1959	Lemass: Fianna Fail (De Valera retired)	Fine Gael	IRA/Sinn Fein
1966	Lynch: Fianna Fail (Lemass retired)	Fine Gael	IRA/Sinn Fein
1973	Cosgrave: (Fine Gael) Fine Gael/Labour Coalition	Fianna Fail	Provisional IRA/Sinn Fein (founded 1969)
1977	Lynch: Fianna Fail	Fine Gael	Provisional IRA/Sinn Fein

1979	Haughey: Fianna Fail	Fine Gael	Provisional IRA/Sinn Fein
1981	FitzGerald: Fine Gael	Fianna Fail	Provisional IRA/Sinn Fein
Mar.–Dec. 1982	Haughey: Fianna Fail	Fine Gael	Provisional IRA/Sinn Fein
1982	FitzGerald: Fine Gael/Labour Coalition	Fianna Fail	Provisional IRA/Sinn Fein
1987	Haughey: Fianna Fail	Fine Gael	Provisional IRA/Sinn Fein

A system of proportional representation was established by the Government of Ireland Act 1920 and this was continued in the Free State and later constitutions. Because of this, there have always been significant numbers of TDs who are members of small parties or who sit as Independents. Labour Party seats in the Dail have varied generally between ten and twenty. In 1959, and again in 1968, a referendum was held on whether to introduce the British 'first past the post' system of elections. On both occasions there was a majority in favour of keeping proportional representation. The number of seats in the Dail has been increased from 128 in 1922 to 166.

The Sinn Fein Party remaining after the formation of Fianna Fail refused to recognise both the Dublin and Belfast governments since they were established by the Government of Ireland Act and the Treaty. Sinn Fein did not take any part in elections, and was regarded as being the political voice of the IRA. In 1969 the IRA/Sinn Fein leaders proposed that they should recognise the Irish and British Governments in Dublin and Belfast 'de facto' – that is, they could be accepted as existing in fact if not by right. This was opposed by the majority of members, who broke away to form the Provisional IRA/Sinn Fein which is now the larger and more active group.

Appendix II
Northern Ireland Prime Ministers:
Unionist Party

Craig	1921–1940
Andrews	1940–1943
Brooke	1943–1963
O'Neill	1963–1969
Chichester–Clark	1969–1971
Faulkner	1971–1972 (Stormont Parliament suspended)

Index

Acknowledgements

We are indebted to Methuen & Co Ltd for permission to reproduce a letter in *Ireland under the Union* by P.S. O'Hegarty.
Short extracts taken from: page 3, *The Illustrated London News*, August 1848; pages 13 and 14, James Carty (ed.), *Ireland from Grattan's Parliament to the Great Famine*, E.J. Fallon 1949; page 30, P.S. O'Hegarty, *Ireland under the Union*, Methuen 1952; page 53, Dan Breen, *My Fight for Irish Freedom*, Anvil Books 1964; page 58, D. Macardle, *The Irish Republic*, Corgi 1968; page 102, T. O'Neill, *The Autobiography of Terence O'Neill*, Rupert Hart Davis 1972.

We are grateful to the following for permission to reproduce photographs: BBC Hulton Picture Library, page 15; *Belfast Telegraph*, page 85; British Library, pages 10, 67, 69, 81, 88; Philip Byrne, page 41; Jim Connolly Photography, page 81; Educational Company of Ireland, a trading unit of Smurfit Ireland Limited, pages 1, 42; Fotocraft, Dublin, page 79; *Illustrated London News* Picture Library, pages 35, 46, 53, 60, 72; The Keystone Collection, page 76; (R18427), 18 (Lawrence Collection, I506), 23 (Lawrence Collection, R2410), 25, 54 (R12169); Pacemaker Press International, page 91; Public Record Office of Northern Ireland, page 37; Radio Telefis Eireann: The Cashman Collection, page 51; Rex Features, page 94; Ulster Museum, pages 4, 13, 20, 32.

Cover: Cartoon. "The Fight For the Banner" by Leonard Raven-Hill, from *Punch*, 15 April, 1914.